Rajmata Gayatri Devi...
Enduring Grace

PAUL
HESSE

Family Pride
Series

Rajmata Gayatri Devi...
Enduring Grace

Dharmendar Kanwar

Lustre Press
Roli Books

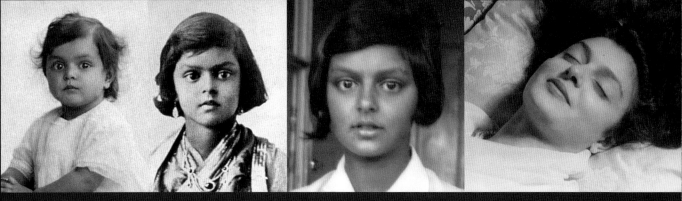

ISBN: 978-81-7436-295-7

Text: © Dharmendar Kanwar 2004
Foreword: © Maharaja Gaj Singh II
Photographs: © Sawai Jai Singh Benevolent Trust and
The De Beers Collection

This edition Roli & Janssen BV 2011
Third impression
Published in India by
Roli Books in arrangement with
Roli & Janssen BV, The Netherlands
M-75 Greater Kailash-II Market
New Delhi-110 048, India.
Phone: ++91-11-40682000
Fax: ++91-11-29217185
Email: info@rolibooks.com
Website: www.rolibooks.com
Printed and bound in Singapore

Contents

Foreword

Rajmata Gayatri Devi remains for all of us the enduring symbol of an age gone by; of a way of life that is already history... Yet, the fairy tale image does not do full justice to the person I have had the privilege of knowing well for many years now. As a contemporary and close friend of her son, the late Maharaja Jagat Singh, I spent many memorable days with them, and realized that there was much more to her beyond her grace, charm and elegance: there was a rare spirit and courage befitting a Rajput Maharani. She was never 'a glass doll' as Indira Gandhi had once described her, which is why she was able to withstand the high and low tides of life.

A trendsetter from the very beginning, Princess Gayatri Devi came to her own as the Maharani of Jaipur in 1940 shortly before turning twenty-one. According to an article of those time, '...the new Maharani is doing unimaginable things: she has started going to the kitchens and supervising them [the cooks]; she was on the fields and playing badminton and tennis; she bobbed her hair, wore slacks, watched polo ... and could be seen riding, not only in the palace grounds, but alongside the Maharaja ...' In all this, as she had once told me, she had been gently encouraged by her husband, the late Maharaja of Jaipur, Sawai Man Singh II, a man known to have been ahead of his times. He also assigned his young bride the special task of emancipating women in Jaipur State, and of bringing them out of the purdah. While this was not the easiest or most coveted mission, it was the most perfectly suited to the young Maharani.

The Maharani Gayatri Devi Girls School was started in 1943 with twenty-one students. Today, as it celebrates its Diamond Jubilee year, it is one of the finest girls' schools in the country with students from almost every state and community on its alumni list. I remember it served as a model when we were mulling over the idea of a sister school for Mayo College. Even today, as its founder, she continues to play a very important part in its activities: the school bears the unmistakable stamp of her personality.

Not content with the singular success of the Maharani Gayatri Devi Girls School, she set up other educational institutions, each unique in its own field—Maharaja Sawai Man Singh Vidyalaya, popularly known as SMS, the Lalitya Bal Niketan and the Sawai Ram Singh Shilp Kala Mandir. The famous Jaipur Blue Pottery and local dari craft owe their revival to her in no small measure.

Maharani, wife, social reformer, international celebrity…she has been all this and more with inimitable panache.

In 1947 with the difficult Accession; in 1949 with the complicated Merger; in 1956 with the inevitable reorganization when the late His Highness relinquished the position of the Rajpramukh, and later became the Ambassador to Spain…it was perhaps the worst of times, and the best of times.

The early sixties ushered in a brave and bold new chapter in her life. As a member of the opposition Swatantra Party, she won a seat in Parliament with a world record-breaking majority.

History will provide an answer to why Rajaji's Swatantra Party experiment failed; but in 1970 a personal tragedy befell Maharani Gayatri Devi—her beloved husband passed away in England. She went through the experience with quiet dignity and deep resolve—like a Maharani.

In 1971, this time as the Rajmata of Jaipur, she was re-elected to Parliament, but on the eve of very difficult times. Later in the year, the Princes were derecognized; and in 1975 (many have seen this as an inevitable outcome), Emergency was declared in the country. In July 1975, the Rajmata, still a conscientious MP, was arrested for some ridiculous tax irregularity. The arrest reeked of political vendetta, and she was sent to the Tihar Jail in Delhi along with the present Maharaja of Jaipur, Sawai Bhawani Singh MVC. We were horrified and outraged when we heard the news. But once again, she took everything in her stride, with dignity…

Aunty Ayesha is truly 'A Princess to be Remembered'.

Maharaja Gajsingh II

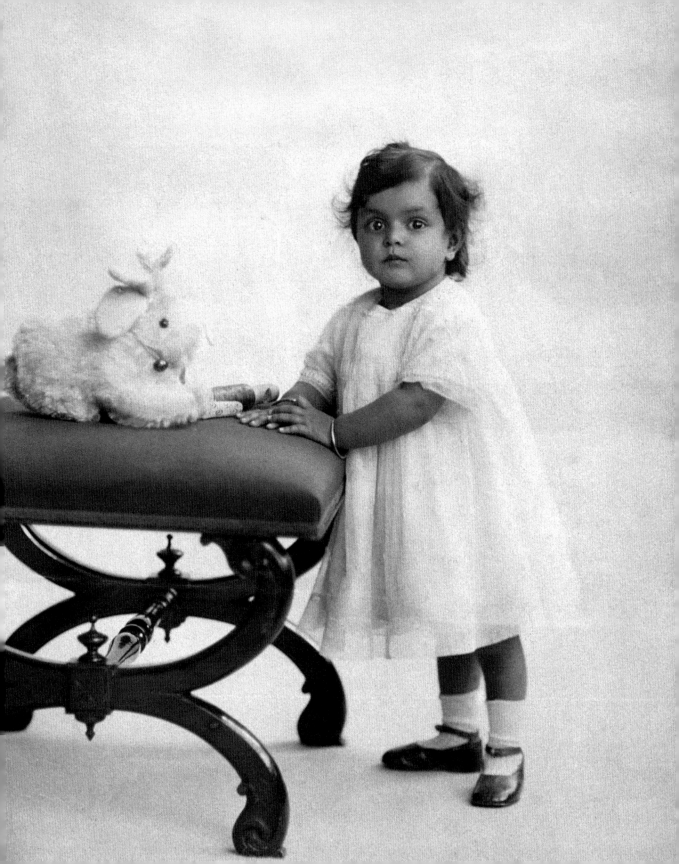

Childhood:
The Early Years

There is a garden in every childhood, an enchanted place where the colours are brighter, the air softer, and the morning more fragrant than ever again.

—Elizabeth Laurence

S he came from a family of good-looking people—her parents and her other siblings had their share of good looks too. As children nobody was really bothered about beauty nor did they give it too much importance. In their younger days, it was mostly always the exquisitely beautiful Princess Ayesha who was much written about, so much so that not many people today know that her mother, Princess Indira Devi Gaekwar, was also an extremely attractive woman. Rajmata herself recalls, 'I find it so difficult even now to talk about my mother's beauty. We just took her looks for granted. I do remember, however, that my resemblance to her was quite striking because the Viceroy, Lord Irvin used to call me Second Her Highness. She was, without doubt, one of the most amazingly beautiful and exciting women that I have known.'

The good-looking Princess Indira Devi Gaekwar was the only daughter of the benevolent and enlightened Maharaja Sayaji Rao III Gaekwar and Maharani Chimnabai of Baroda. A true Maratha at

Princess Ayesha when she was barely a year old.

FACING PAGE:

A shutterbug's delight.

The little Princess Ayesha would grow up to be one of the most photographed women in the world.

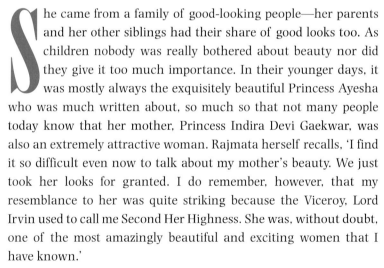

heart and in her upbringing, Princess Indira Devi inherited several qualities from her parents and, like them, was quite modern in her outlook. Her English education also made her fiercely independent in her thinking.

In 1911, the Maharaja Scindia of Gwalior—Gwalior was one of the most important Maratha states in princely India—asked for Indira Devi's hand in marriage. Her father was very pleased at the thought of marrying her into a family befitting the state of Baroda. She was engaged to the Maharaja for almost a year and even went trousseau shopping in England before she decided that she couldn't go ahead with the marriage.

She wrote to her fiancé that she did not wish to marry him. He in turn wrote to Princess Indira Devi's father and sought an explanation. Rajmata says, 'My mother was unhappy with this arranged marriage even before she had met and fallen in love with my father. Charming as he was, the Maharaja Scindia of Gwalior was also twenty years older than her and a very conservative man. She feared that marrying him would mean spending the rest of her life confined to the great palace of Gwalior. Being an educated and well-travelled eighteen-year-old girl this rigid and confining form of the purdah was a very uninviting prospect. She caused a major upheaval when she announced to her parents that she could not marry the Maharaja because she had fallen in love with Maharaj Kumar Jitendra Narayan Bhup Bahadur of

Cooch Behar, a young prince from the east whom she had met in 1911 at the Delhi Durbar.'

There was a lot of opposition from the family. Cooch Behar was a smaller state and the rulers were not Marathas. More importantly, the Cooch Behars were known in the country to be Westernized in their ways.

The young princess, however, married her dashing prince in England in 1913, two years after she had met him.

'The family continued to put pressure on my mother but she had her way after all and when she went to say goodbye to her mother, the Maharani sat stony-faced and showed no sign of affection. But when her sobbing daughter left the room the Maharani broke down and wept as though her heart would break. My grandmother could look extremely stern but beneath lay a heart of gold,' says Rajmata of her maternal grandmother.

Maharaj Kumari Gayatri Devi, better known as Princess Ayesha, was the fourth of five children born to Maharani Indira Devi and Maharaja Jitendra Narayan Bhup Bahadur of Cooch Behar. Unfortunately, the Maharaja did not live long enough to see his children grow up. He died of pneumonia in 1922, in England, nine years after his marriage. Maharani Indira Devi or Ma Cooch Behar was a strong woman and when she lost her husband she returned to India with her five children and made arrangements to install her seven-year-old son, Jagaddipendra Narayan as the new Maharaja of Cooch Behar. In those days it was customary to appoint a Regent and Minority Council. Hence it was hardly surprising or unusual when Ma Cooch Behar herself was appointed the Regent. She took her role very seriously and guided her young son through the duties of the state.

'We were a very close-knit family. I had a very happy and carefree childhood. Each one of us had the freedom to do what we wanted. We learnt how to ride, play tennis and cricket with the best coaches possible. There are so many stories connected to my childhood...' Maharaj Kumari Ila Devi was born in 1914 in Calcutta. 'Ila was the

Inheriting the mother's good looks.

Princess Indira Devi, Gayatri Devi's mother, as a young girl.

FACING PAGE:

Mother and grandmother.

Princess Indira Devi's mother Maharani Chimnabai of Baroda was always encouraged by her husband to champion the cause of women in India. She went on to become the President of the All India Women's Conference.

11

Baroda grandfather with family.

Maharaja Sayaji Rao III Gaekwar was a ruler well ahead of his times. A much-respected Maharaja, he had hired tutors to teach his wife, Maharani Chimnabai, to read and write. The couple is seen here with their son and daughter outside the Baroda Palace.

BOTTOM:

Maharani Indira Devi.

Maharani Indira Devi was known in India and Europe for the lavish parties that she hosted.

oldest, and the witty one. She was good at riding and tennis, and was an excellent mimic. I also remember that she used to tease me a lot. Yuvraj Jagaddipendra Narayan, better known as Bhaiya, was born in 1915 in Cooch Behar. Bhaiya was tall, good-looking and full of fun. I simply adored him and remember how once he gave me a green thing to eat and said it was a sweet. That was the first time I tasted a green chilli and I just screamed and screamed.' Maharaj Kumar Indrajitendra Narayan was born in 1918 in Poona. 'Indrajit was the mischievous one and used to spend his days getting into one of a dozen different sorts of trouble.'

Maharaj Kumari Gayatri Devi was born in England on 23 May, 1919 and a year later, in 1920, Maharaj Kumari Menaka Devi, the youngest sibling was born. 'Menaka looked shy because she was quiet but she was really very sociable and also had a great sense of humour. While I was more of a tomboy, she was very ladylike and loved dressing up and wearing jewels,' recalls Rajmata looking back on those happy years of her childhood.

12

Ma Cooch Behar.

Ma Cooch Behar was a beauty, petite and charming. Widowed at the young age of thirty, after only nine years of marriage, she brought up five children on her own. She was the first major influence on the young Gayatri Devi.

LEFT:

Portrait of Ma Cooch Behar.

This portrait of the stunning Ma Cooch Behar occupies the pride of place in the drawing room at Lilypool, Rajmata's present residence.

Mother, sister and brother.

Ma with her two older children, Maharaj Kumari Ila Devi and Maharaj Kumar Jagaddipendra Narayan, in England.

Royal baby in a London studio.

Princess Ayesha, the royal baby, was photographed in a London studio. Portraits were an indispensable part of growing up in a royal household.

'Oh, we had our usual fights,' smiles Menaka Devi, now eighty-two-years old. 'Nothing serious, just arguments about not allowing each other to touch our respective toys. She never bullied me or pushed me around. We had a doll's house in the rear grounds of the Cooch Behar Palace where all of us played for hours.'

There is an interesting story on how Rajmata came to be called 'Ayesha'. 'Friends used to question my mother about my Muslim name but I was called Ayesha simply because my mother had been reading H. Rider Haggard's novel *She* when she was expecting me and had already decided that if a girl was born she would name her Ayesha, after the heroine of the book. There was no other reason behind it. Since I was born in England, my horoscope was cast in India after the time difference had been calculated by the pundits, and the auspicious letter "G" was selected for my name,' smiles Rajmata.

The Cooch Behars travelled to England frequently and going back to those early years Rajmata says, 'As children, I remember, we attended many schools—in England, Switzerland and then in India.' The first school was Glendower, a day school in London where Rajmata and her younger sister Menaka Devi were the only Indian pupils.

Ma Cooch Behar was the first and the most enduring influence on Rajmata because she remembers very little about her father. She was barely three years old when he passed away but does recall that Ma had a very busy social life. Ma was to be seen at all the stylish casinos across Europe. She also had a great reputation for entertaining and threw the most lavish parties that became the talk of the town. Ma was a stunningly beautiful woman and Rashid Ali

14

The Cooch Behar family in England.

The Cooch Behars travelled quite frequently to England. In fact, Gayatri Devi was born in England in 1919. The Cooch Behars sent their children to schools in England, Switzerland and India.

TOP:

Princess Ayesha and her siblings.

The Cooch Behar children with their newly-born sister, Menaka Devi.

RIGHT:

Sisters.

Ila Devi, the eldest and wittiest of the lot, with the youngest sibling Menaka Devi.

Baig, a close friend and son of Sir Mirza Ali Baig, a friend of her father, wrote in his autobiography: 'To describe her beauty as ravishing would by no means be using an overworked cliché. Reporters flocked to our home (she was married from our home in London), endless photographs were taken and we small boys lived in a haze of reflected glory.'

The Cooch Behar children had an amazing childhood. 'You must understand that given my mother's lifestyle there was a fair amount of shifting that was necessary. For instance, when she felt that my brother needed to go to a school where he could grow up without being treated like a Maharaj Kumar she consulted the Viceroy who suggested that he be sent to England. Though we stayed back in India

TOP LEFT:

A special occasion.

Princess Ayesha dressed in royal finery for a portrait session.

TOP RIGHT:

Father and brother.

Gayatri Devi's father Maharaja Jitendra Narayan Bhup Bahadur passed away when she was very small. Here he is seen with his eldest son Maharaj Kumar Jagaddipendra Narayan Bhup Bahadur, then a mere toddler.

TOP:

Gayatri Devi at nine.

Tutors were hired to teach various subjects to the royal children.

LEFT:

At a shooting camp.

Gayatri Devi and her mother enjoy a meal with family friends at a shooting camp.

FACING PAGE:

At the age of ten.

She was already as stunning as Ma Cooch Behar

and spent most of our summer months in Darjeeling and Ooty, we also went to England during my brother's summer vacations. It was not as if we were travelling all the time but it was easier for us to go to England. We were educated mainly in Cooch Behar because we were being given lessons by our two governesses Miss Hobart and Miss Olyphant (who later started the Welham's School in Dehradun) and also had tutors for other subjects. This ensured that we were never lacking in our regular lessons. So the question of being in a strange place never really bothered us. However, many a times I did wish that I didn't have to go to so many schools,' recalls Rajmata.

In 1929 Menaka Devi fell ill and had to be sent to a sanatorium at Leysin, in Switzerland. Gayatri Devi and Baby, daughter of General Khusro Jung, the guardian of the five Cooch Behar children, went to a nearby school called Les Noisetiers.

Those were enjoyable days. Hesky Baig, nephew of General Khusro Jung, was a childhood friend of Gayatri Devi. He, along with his cousin Baby, grew up with the Cooch Behar children. After Partition he moved to Pakistan but the links were never severed. 'The end of World War II and the creation of Pakistan made no difference to our

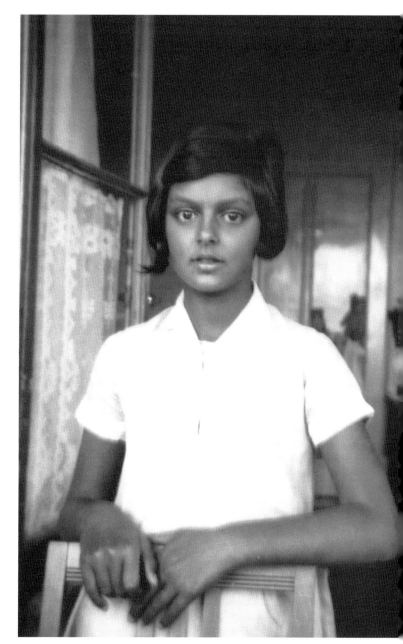

At the airport.

The family often took trips by air. The children especially enjoyed travelling together, and were often accompanied by their friends.

In Engleberg, Switzerland.

Gayatri Devi did her finishing school in Switzerland.

feelings or association, except that our meetings became more infrequent and had to be carefully planned. England became the venue of our family gatherings,' wrote Hesky Baig in an article for *The Star* in 1983. 'We had great fun. We hunted with the Beaufort hounds, attended horse shows and country fairs. Ayesha, always in the forefront of our communal activities, was growing into a beautiful and cultured woman.'

Rajmata also remembers her mother's role in doing up the palace in Cooch Behar and all their other homes. 'She excelled in decorating and arranging the house and we had the most beautiful homes in Cooch Behar, Calcutta and Darjeeling. She loved collecting *objets d'art* wherever she went. There was furniture from

England and France, fabric and chandeliers from Italy, rugs from Kashmir and so on. She had great style and how we lived was a reflection of her taste and personality.'

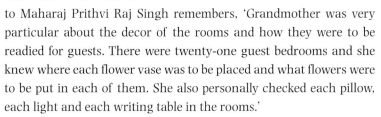

Devika Devi, Ila Devi's daughter and also Rajmata's daughter-in-law who was married to Maharaj Prithvi Raj Singh remembers, 'Grandmother was very particular about the decor of the rooms and how they were to be readied for guests. There were twenty-one guest bedrooms and she knew where each flower vase was to be placed and what flowers were to be put in each of them. She also personally checked each pillow, each light and each writing table in the rooms.'

Ma was an incredible woman and handled her duties and responsibilities admirably. It couldn't have been an easy job looking after five children and attending to matters of the state.

The children were also fortunate enough to have the huge Cooch Behar Palace to play in and they put it to very good use. Sprawling grounds surrounded the Cooch Behar Palace where the girls had their own wing, with enough rooms to play and study in, while the boys had a separate wing to themselves. There were fields for cricket, hockey and football, one squash and three tennis courts. Riding was out in the country.

The Archaeological Survey of India (ASI) has now acquired the palace and is in the process of turning it into a museum. Rajmata continues to take keen interest in it and advises the officers concerned whenever she visits her home state every year. Just outside the palace are hawkers selling picture postcards of the family and their home. During a visit to the palace in 2001, officials

TOP:

Parents and brothers.

Maharaja Sayaji Rao III Gaekwar, with his daughter Maharani Indira Devi and her two sons, Maharaj Kumar Jagaddipendra Narayan Bhup Bahadur and Maharaj Kumar Indrajitendra Narayan Bhup Bahadur, in London during a summer break.

21

*The Cooch Behars spend a
leisurely day in the countryside.*

from the ASI there
happily showed her the
repair work that had
been carried out since
her previous visit. She
went from one room
to another sometimes
stopping at a particular
spot and pondering for a
while. 'This is where we
had our tuitions. This was the room that I shared with Menaka.'
Even in its present dilapidated condition, it is an impressive palace
and she has vivid memories of it. 'We had a very large bedroom and
the mosquito net-covered beds were placed almost in the centre of
the room. The walls had beautiful blue, white and yellow

Brothers and sisters.

The brothers and sisters shared a very close relationship, and had great fun when they gathered in Cooch Behar. Seldom was there a boring moment because their mother was a splendid hostess and had guests over throughout the year.

Fancy dress party in Cooch Behar.

Friends and relatives came to Cooch Behar Palace either to spend their holidays, or to go for picnics and shikars, or just to have fun. Fancy dress parties were very popular and organized quite often.

24

marguerites painted on them. There was also a sofa and upholstered armchairs.'

They also had their governesses, personal maids, ADCs and valets. 'Much has been written about the number of staff that we had but it was a huge palace and people were needed to maintain it. There were gardeners, stable hands, sweepers, guards, people to look after the elephants and of course the countless guests who visited regularly.'

The palace holds a lot of happy memories for her. 'We had the most wonderful childhood possible, there was so much activity there, so many young cousins and a constant stream of visitors,' says Rajmata with a faraway look in her eyes, transported back into an idyllic past, as it were.

TOP AND FACING PAGE TOP:
Riding in Cooch Behar.
Gayatri Devi was an expert rider and still nutures a great passion for horses.

FACING PAGE MIDDLE:
The sharpshooter.
She shot her first panther at the age of twelve in Cooch Behar.

FACING PAGE BOTTOM:
Game bird.
On a duck shoot with Rao Raja Abhay Singh's daughter.

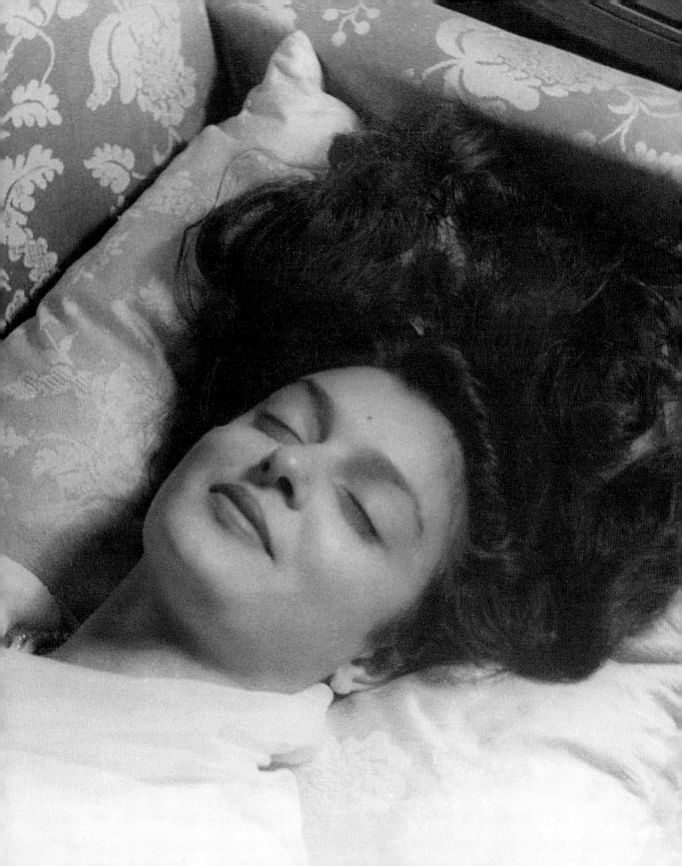

Growing Up
in Wonderland

To live is to be slowly born.

—Antoine de Saint-Exupery

Ma had heard about Gurudev Rabindranath Tagore's school Shantiniketan. She felt that the girls had had enough of Western education and wanted them to be able to converse in their mother tongue Bengali. She felt that Shantiniketan would the best place for them to imbibe the traditional Indian values and culture that was necessary for them.

In July 1934, the girls set off for Shantiniketan. It was an altogether new experience for them; they were in a totally Indian ambience, closer to their roots. It was a change but not one that the young princesses could not adjust to. 'It wasn't as if we were fully Westernized. We were brought up in Cooch Behar and our mother ensured that we never lost touch with our traditions. In fact she even went to the extent of encouraging us to have a bath with a *lota* (brass vessel) and *balti* (bucket).'

An ADC, his family and a maid accompanied them. Gayatri Devi slept in the dormitory with the other girls and was there for almost a year. She recalls those days with great fondness. 'There were two girls from Bihar named Amla and Vimla who used to help me with Mathematics. There was Shantiji who was much older than us, and a mother of five children. She wanted to get through her matriculation so that she could get a good job. There was Renu who was on the bed

FACING PAGE AND TOP:

Schooldays.

After having schooled in England and Switzerland, Gayatri Devi was sent to Shantiniketan to imbibe Indian culture.

next to mine and always irritated me during exam time because her alarm would go off every hour or so and she would switch on the light and start studying. Once when I was just about to take her photograph she said, "Wait! Wait!" and quickly ran in and put on some perfume. She wanted to send a copy of the photograph to her husband!'

Gurudev was a much respected and revered figure and was always there in the background watching over the school. 'I used to borrow somebody's bicycle and whenever I had a free moment I would go and see Gurudev,' says Rajmata of her Shantiniketan days. 'To me he represented the rest of the world, as it was outside. He was a well-known person and he used to travel a lot. I had great regard for him. In my rare meetings with him he gently encouraged me to pursue dancing and participate in more ladylike activities. I had to drop out of dancing because it clashed with my tennis timings. I preferred tennis to dancing!'

Before marriage in Srinagar.

Maharani Indira Devi often took the family to Srinagar in summer. Other friends also joined them there. During one such trip, Gayatri Devi spends a quiet moment by herself.

28

Gayatri Devi returning to India after spending the summer months in England.

In March 1936, almost a year after joining Shantiniketan, Gayatri Devi left for Cooch Behar to take her matriculation exam. She passed with a First Class. Schooling over, Ma decided to send her off to a finishing school in Switzerland.

Ma had many polo-playing friends and one of them was the dashing Maharaja of Jaipur—Maharaja Sawai Man Singh II. Their mutual interest in horses had him visiting the Cooch Behars whenever he was in Calcutta to play polo. Sometimes he even visited them in England if they happened to be there during the polo season. He had grown quite close to Ma in the 1920s when, as a teenager growing up in Ooty he asked to be invited over to their summer house for Indian food. The contact was kept alive in England as well when he attended parties thrown by Ma. She was a much written about and photographed society lady in Europe of the 1930s. This twice-married Maharaja came from a state where women were always in

29

the purdah and not used to socializing with men. He was very impressed with the glamorous, educated and beautiful Ma Cooch Behar. She was unlike any woman he had met and for him she was somebody he looked up to for advice on various matters.

The Cooch Behars were like a family to Maharaja Man Singh and had much in common with him. Like him, they were exposed to the Western way of life having spent a lot of time in Europe. They were equally sophisticated and provided the kind of companionship he yearned for. Besides his close ties with Ma, Maharaja Man Singh was also a great friend of Bhaiya, Gayatri Devi's older brother, and was fond of the other children as well.

Gayatri Devi hero-worshipped Maharaja Man Singh. He in turn had made up his mind that he would marry the fourteen-year-old princess when she was older. When he conveyed this to Ma she didn't take him seriously and said that she had never heard such sentimental rubbish! Gayatri Devi was too young and Ma did not think that the Maharaja would really continue to be interested in her teenaged daughter for long.

She hoped that the finishing school in Switzerland would keep her daughter's mind occupied and, if possible, take her far away from

Carefree days.

Gayatri Devi was only fourteen years old when Maharaja Man Singh decided to marry her once she was older.

this business of falling in love. Ma's efforts were in vain. The young girl continued to be attracted to 'Jai'.

Rajmata smiles as she recalls the years of her first meetings with the Maharaja of Jaipur. 'When he first came to Woodlands, our home in Calcutta, in December 1931, my first impression of him was an impeccably dressed, glamorous, slim and handsome young man. In my sports-loving eyes he was especially glamorous as he was India's leading polo player.'

In 1936 Ma took her family to Europe. Gayatri Devi's maternal grandmother took Ila and Menaka with her by ship. Gayatri Devi and Ma followed them later by air.

Just before leaving, Ma got the news that Ila had already married

With the German Baroness in London.

The German Baroness used to look after the sisters when they were studying in Europe.

31

a cousin of the Maharaja of Tripura. His name was Romendra Kishore Dev Burman, and he had been her fellow student at Shantiniketan. She had married him secretly on 12 June 1936 before returning to Cooch Behar.

Shocked and hurt Ma could not reconcile herself to the fact that her daughter had been so defiant. She did remember that she too had married against her parents' wishes but at least she had informed them and they had made the arrangements for the marriage. How could a princess marry in so underhand and undignified a manner? She could only question Ila once she got to Paris and had to hold her peace until then.

When Gayatri Devi and Ma landed in Paris a showdown was inevitable. Ma and Ila met. There were a lot of heated arguments. In the end, however, the result was exactly what Ila had hoped for—a proper marriage would be arranged when they returned to India.

TOP:

Skiing with friends.

Schooldays at Les Noisetiers were fun with lots of other interesting activities packed in. Skiing was one of them.

SECOND FROM TOP:

Always game.

Gayatri Devi's passion for horses was doubled with her enthusiasm for big game hunting.

The first few weeks were spent in hectic shopping for Ila's trousseau. From there both mother and daughter went to London to continue shopping. Gayatri Devi still had four months to finish school in Switzerland and Ma did not wish to let her sit around doing nothing. So when a friend recommended a finishing school called the Monkey Club to fill in the gap, Ma enrolled her girls there. They lived in Pont Street and were under the watchful eyes of Maharani Chimnabai, their Baroda grandmother, and a German Baroness.

'My mother was a great friend of Ma and she was the one who recommended the Monkey Club to her,' says Lady Kennard. 'In fact, I was already enrolled there when Ayesha came and since we had known each other earlier, we just continued spending a lot of time together.'

Lady Kennard, a niece of Lord Mountbatten, is a regular visitor to Jaipur and one of Rajmata's few surviving school friends. 'We used to talk about almost everything under the sun. We had a wonderful time there and I do remember that she used to say that she would

With sister Menaka in Switzerland.

Gayatri Devi with sister Menaka Devi ice skating in Switzerland.

marry the Maharaja of Jaipur. When I said she couldn't because she would have to stay in the purdah, she said, "No, I'm not going to be in any purdah."' Purdah was not an issue that bothered her too much. She knew what 'Jai' felt about it and she knew she would have his support even after marriage.

Maharaja Man Singh was a regular visitor to England and continued to meet Gayatri Devi as often as he could, and her days were spent meeting him on the sly and spending as much time with him as she could. This was possible because Ma had to return to Cooch Behar to organize a proper wedding for her elder daughter Ila Devi. The younger Maharaj Kumaris Menaka Devi and Gayatri Devi stayed on in England with their grandmother. It was now easier to steal away and meet the dashing Maharaja. Just before it was time for Gayatri Devi to leave for finishing school at Brillantmont in Lausanne, she went to say goodbye to Maharaja Man Singh. They went for a drive around Hyde Park when 'Jai' proposed to her. The sixteen-year-old princess didn't bat an eyelid before agreeing to marry her prince charming. Maharaja Man Singh was a little taken aback at this spontaneous and instant acquiescence and wanted to give her time to make up her mind. She had never been surer of her mind as she was then. She didn't want any time and she didn't want to think again!

It now became necessary to meet everyday. And meet they did despite the heavy protection and vigilance of her guardians. She remembers the phone calls; the elaborate plans to sneak out on dates without her chaperones finding out anything. The courtship was great fun because of the secrecy involved and the fact that it was conducted without the approval of her mother. When Gayatri Devi and Maharaja Man Singh could not be together, they wrote to each other expressing their feelings and their desire to be together again.

Playing tennis.

The Maharani thoroughly enjoyed a good game of tennis and played mainly with male partners as hardly any woman in Jaipur could play the game.

Falling in Love

A touch of love,
everyone becomes a poet.

—Plato

It was just a matter of time before Ma was informed. Maharaja Man Singh told Gayatri Devi to write to her mother about having accepted his proposal. Gayatri Devi was nervous realizing what a difficult job that was. 'I just could not bring myself to compose a letter to my mother saying that I had decided to marry Jai and that she should agree to it, so I kept putting it off.'

Her delay in writing confused Maharaja Man Singh and he was worried that she may have changed her mind. Finding herself in a bit of a fix, she appealed to an old family friend, Dr Chandrachud, who happened to be in Lausanne with her maternal grandfather, to help her out of her predicament. Together they composed the letter and Gayatri Devi informed her mother that she had agreed to marry the Maharaja of Jaipur because he had asked her and because she wanted to!

As expected, her mother wrote back advising that they wait for a few years and see how they feel about each other and then decide. Time flew by. Meanwhile Maharaja Man Singh had an accident while playing polo and had to go to Vienna for an operation. After his two-week convalescence, he went to Lausanne to see Gayatri Devi at her finishing school. She told the school authorities that he was a cousin and went out with him. That Maharaja Man Singh's pictures appeared in the gossip columns and that she was questioned closely about him is quite another story. All her mail was opened thereafter.

FACING PAGE:

In Spanish hues.

This portrait was done in Spain where Maharaja Man Singh had been sent on an ambassadorial mission by the government of India. Maharani Gayatri Devi found everything about Spain fascinating except that the Spaniards spoke too fast.

BOTTOM:

A princess in love.

It was love at first sight for the young Princess Ayesha. 'Jai' was in every way the man that she had dreamt of.

Rajmata remembers the Principal of the finishing school very well. 'She was called Madame Heubi and she did make an impression on me. She was quite strict and I remember when I broke bounds one day she gently reprimanded me and said, "You shouldn't have done this." I said that this was not a regular school but just a finishing school. She said that life itself was a school and that the process of learning never really ends. Somehow, I've always remembered that and it is so true.'

Life at the finishing school was enjoyable. 'Marlene Dietrich's daughter was also in school with me. I was the first Indian girl there and my first friends were English and American because we had a language in common but later on I made a lot of friends.' She especially enjoyed skiing and other sporting activities and remembers the time when she had to pack a trunk to go up to the mountains for skiing.

'I hadn't packed in my life before and just looked at the box wondering what to do with it! As I sat on the bed looking dazed, one of the girls came up to me and asked me what was wrong. I told her that I had a slight headache. She suggested I lie down, and then started to pack my trunk. I was quite relieved and watched her pack shoes at the bottom, then the skiing clothes, and finally the saris on top.'

After Brillantmont, Maharaja Man Singh was afraid that if the princess returned to India she would suddenly find herself getting engaged to someone chosen by her elders. Gayatri Devi too decided that she did not wish to return to India just as yet. With encouragement from Maharaja Man Singh and her mother's approval, she joined the London College of Secretaries. While the evenings were spent visiting friends, 'Miss Devi' spent the mornings learning amidst other things shorthand, typing, accounting, book-keeping.

The princess picked up a lot of useful skills at the London College of Secretaries but unlike the other students she wasn't looking for a job. 'I remember feeling a little embarrassed when I was asked about the kind of job I was looking for. I could hardly say that I

was a princess and that I didn't really need a job. Most of the girls
there were from a working-class background. I really had no clue just
how and where I would use the skills. All I could think of saying was
that my mother had a lot of work to do so I would probably be doing
her secretarial work. However, what was good about those days was
the fact that I could interact with ordinary people. Even after they
learnt about me from the newspapers, they were very matter-of-fact
about it and took it in their stride as if having a princess learning how
to type was an everyday event in that college,' says Rajmata.

A fairy-tale romance.

*On their visits to England and
Germany, Gayatri Devi and
Maharaja Man Singh would
meet clandestinely before they
were finally married*

40

Ma was still hoping that both Maharaja Man Singh and her daughter would get over this attraction. It wasn't as if she considered the Maharaja of Jaipur to be ineligible in any way at all. In fact she had great regard for him and was very fond of him. Friends and relatives warned Ma that her daughter's life as the third Maharani of Maharaja Man Singh would be very difficult. Not only was Ma worried about her daughter having to become a third wife, but as someone who had grown quite fond of Maharaja Man Singh's second wife, Kishore Kanwar, Ma did not want her to be hurt by this alliance.

'His Highness used to say that I was so young and childish that I would be spending most of my time in the nursery!' smiles Rajmata. The two young people were determined to marry and didn't think that Ma needed to nurse her doubts and fears. They continued to meet each other and correspond regularly. They had their usual lovers' tiffs but their love story progressed satisfactorily. Rajmata remembers sneaking out to the phone booth on Pont Street (it is still there) to talk to Maharaja Man Singh.

'It was so important to be able to talk to Jai without somebody eavesdropping each time. I used to go to this small cubicle where I would try to conceal myself while making my phone calls! Very often he would ask me out and I would happily agree. In order to hide the fact that we were meeting regularly, Jai would park his Bentley in Wilton Crescent, I would walk to that place, get into the waiting car and we would drive off!

'Those times were much more fun than an ordinary approved courtship would have been. We were constantly trying to outsmart our elders, arranging clandestine meetings and finding a system of posting letters to each other without our ADCs and other staff getting any wiser. Once in a while we also managed to go boating and on long drives in the country and have dinner at Bray. We formalized our relationship by buying gold rings with our names engraved on the inner surface. I, of course, had to save my pocket money to be able to buy one for Jai. It was a lovely and intoxicating time.'

Bhaiya.

Bhaiya or Maharaj Kumar Jagaddipendra Narayan Bhup Bahadur became the Maharaja of Cooch Behar in 1922. He was educated in Harrow and Trinity College in England. A keen polo player and a good friend of Maharaja Man Singh, Bhaiya was a very popular figure at parties, and a highly decorated officer in the Rajendra Hazari Guards of the Jaipur State Forces. He later took over as the Chief Commandant of the Cooch Behar Military Forces.

During the time of the coronation of George VI in 1937, she went to join her mother and brothers in England. A lot of Indian princes were there as well to attend the coronation. Maharaja Man Singh was there with his second wife and their children. Gayatri Devi went over to meet the family with her brother who was a very good friend of Second Her Highness.

Gayatri Devi returned to India in 1938, and spent the first few days in Bombay. Maharaja Man Singh was around and life was good, though a little restricted. She did not have the freedom that she had enjoyed in England where she could go unaccompanied to movies, plays and restaurants. Despite restrictions there was enough scope for the young couple to meet and spend time together. They spent happy times in the Willingdon Club meeting other friends over drinks and at dinner parties.

From Bombay the Cooch Behars and Maharaja Man Singh went on to Calcutta at the peak of the Christmas season. The Cooch Behar boys were in great demand as was the handsome Maharaja Man Singh. The three of them went out together and were the life and soul of the parties that they attended. Menaka Devi says of those days, 'When Bhaiya, Indrajit and His Highness (Maharaja Man Singh) dressed up for formal parties in their uniforms and headgear, they looked so handsome and impressive that we really felt very proud of them.'

The Cooch Behars' own home Woodlands was the hub of social activity with a constant stream of dinners and other get-togethers. For the most part the sprawling grounds had scores of people participating in some event or the other.

Woodlands was sold several years ago and today the entire complex has changed beyond recognition. Several flats and a hospital have completely wiped out all traces of the original house.

When the Cooch Behars lived there, cricket matches were frequently organized since Bhaiya was a keen cricket player. Sometimes tents were pitched in the huge lawns to accommodate cavalry officers who visited Woodlands often to play polo. Life was a

flurry of activities—tennis, riding and watching polo until it was time for the Cooch Behars to go back to Cooch Behar—the real home and a much loved one at that. The country life of Cooch Behar was something that appealed immensely to all of them.

In 1939, Ma decided to move the family to Kashmir during summer, and they stayed on there for eight months. Though it was a temporary residence, she set about furnishing the house with the choicest of carpets, rugs and other *objets d'art*. Other members of the family also moved temporarily to Kashmir. Friends like the Nawab of Pataudi and his wife were amongst those who also moved to Kashmir during summer and added to the social circle. Maharaja Man Singh too came down to Kashmir to spend a few days.

The days of partying were temporarily interrupted with World War II just round the corner. It wasn't long before the men folk started moving back to their states, some to join their units that were preparing to leave for the warfront.

TOP LEFT:

His Highness Maharaja Sawai Man Singh II of Jaipur.
This is one of Rajmata's favourite portraits of the late Maharaja, showing him in the full uniform of the Sawai Man Guards.

TOP RIGHT:

Brother Indrajitendra.
Maharaj Kumar Indrajitendra Narayan Bhup Bahadur was a much-decorated officer of the Central India Horse and served in World War II. He was awarded the Burma, Africa and Pacific stars and Defence, War and IGS medals, and Indian Independence medals.

Marriage

Go confidently in the direction of your dreams.
Live the life you've imagined.

—Henri David Thoreau

Since Gayatri Devi's marriage with Maharaja Man Singh had now been finalized Ma set about ensuring that her daughter had a grand wedding, befitting a princess of Cooch Behar. Astrologers were consulted for an auspicious day and suggested 17 April. The marriage, however, had to be postponed as Ma's favourite brother Maharaj Dhairyashil had an accident and passed away. The astrologers were consulted again and a new date was fixed for the following month. So on 9 May 1940, shortly before her twenty-first birthday Maharaj Kumari Gayatri Devi finally wed her Prince Charming. Cooch Behar was abuzz with activities. The whole township was out on the streets to celebrate the event and local newspapers wrote: 'History Repeats Itself.' Generations ago Maharaja Jai Singh I had also married a princess from Cooch Behar. It did not seem to bother anyone that the present Maharaja of Jaipur already had two wives. His father, Maharaja Sawai Madho Singh had arranged these marriages to princesses from the house of Jodhpur. Maharaja Man Singh was first married to Marudhar Kanwar in 1923 when he was just twelve years old. He married Kishore Kanwar, the niece of the first wife in 1932. And he was marrying for the third time, eight years later.

Gayatri Devi's trousseau came largely from Europe. Ma had ordered towels and sheets from Florence and Czechoslovakia, shoes and matching bags from Ferragamo in Florence, nightgowns in

FACING PAGE:

A long wait.

Maharaja Man Singh and Maharani Gayatri Devi had a seven-year-long courtship before they were finally married.

45

The bridegroom returns.

Maharaja Man Singh is greeted by his nobles on his return to Jaipur from Cooch Behar after the wedding.

mousseline de soie from Paris. The rest of the shopping was done in Calcutta. Gayatri Devi concentrated on her sports gear, and when she was persuaded to buy a few saris, she made a disastrous trip to *Glamour*, a well-known shop of those days, and ordered indiscriminately. The poor shopkeeper was horrified and quickly rang up Ma asking her to come and see her daughter's selection. As expected, Ma rejected all the saris and bought fresh ones.

Ma's choice was impeccable and the princess, as the Maharani of Jaipur, was grateful that her mother had chosen the most appropriate clothing for her.

The kind of saris that Ma had selected for her daughter went on to become a style statement of Rajput women throughout the country. French chiffons in pastels, the head covered gracefully and a string of pearls were considered the hallmark of good dressing and are still associated with Rajmata. However, she recalls, 'People saw me dressed in all those beautiful chiffons and just assumed that I was the one responsible for setting the trend but the credit should go to my

mother. When Ma first saw chiffon in Paris she said that if these could be made 42 inches wide instead of 34 they could be used as saris. The first customers were Nepalese ladies, and then a lot of other ladies also started buying these saris from France. They became quite popular in the years that followed.' But it was certainly the stylish Maharani's personal charisma that popularized that particular look.

The Maharaja of Jaipur came to wed the princess of Cooch Behar in an impressive procession. Forty nobles from his state accompanied him. He arrived on an elephant with horses and dancing girls following him in the marriage procession. He was given a ceremonial welcome as cannons boomed to signal his entry through the gates of the Cooch Behar Palace. On reaching the threshold, he lightly touched the *toran*, or lintel, in a customary gesture to announce the bridegroom's arrival.

The marriage ceremony was an elaborate one with guests dressed in their traditional finery. The puja was a long drawn out one and both Maharaja Man Singh and Maharaj Kumari Gayatri Devi

Maharaja Man Singh arrives at Cooch Behar Palace.

Canons were fired to give Maharaja Man Singh, the bridegroom, a ceremonial welcome at Cooch Behar Palace.

Wedding ceremony.

On 9 May 1940, Maharaja Man Singh took Maharaj Kumari Gayatri Devi of Cooch Behar as his third wife.

FACING PAGE:

The newly weds.

Maharaja Man Singh with his newly wed bride.

were restless though they went through the entire ceremony patiently. The final pujas over, they went to seek the blessings of all the family members.

The marriage celebrations lasted for an entire week with innumerable lunches and dinners thrown in for good measure, and a lot of music and dancing. Maharaja Man Singh and his new bride, Maharani Gayatri Devi, however, joined in the celebrations for only three days.

There was a great deal of sadness in the air when the time came for her to leave her family home. The maids wept, and the sisters and cousins looked forlorn at the thought of their dear sister going away.

Ma Cooch Behar hid her own pain of parting with her daughter under a cloak of indifference which did hurt the young princess but she understood that her mother was still grieving for her brother Maharaj Dhairyashil and needed time to come to terms with his loss and a young daughter's departure.

After the marriage, Maharaja Man Singh and Maharani Gayatri Devi went to Ooty for their honeymoon. They first went to Calcutta, and then took a train to Ooty. As the Maharani of Jaipur, she got a foretaste of things that were to follow. At the station their train coach had been cordoned off with *kanats*, or canvas screens, on both sides so that no other man could set his eyes on her. In fact, to her shock

and discomfiture, this introduction to the purdah started in Calcutta itself when the staff of Jaipur just took over, dismissed all the male servants and kept her cloistered until she boarded the train. She was a little unnerved when her brother whispered to her that he hoped her husband would not keep her so claustrophobically guarded all the time. Though she did not respond at that time, she certainly hoped he wouldn't.

Ooty was fun, with riding, picnics, visiting friends and spending time with each other. The fear of being caught on their earlier clandestine dates was no longer there. They stayed in the annexe of a big house belonging to the Jodhpur royal family. The new Maharani

A memorable occasion.

The gathering at Cooch Behar for Gayatri Devi's wedding with Maharaja Man Singh.

Joey, Bubbles and Pat.

When Gayatri Devi arrived in Jaipur, Maharaja Man Singh already had four children—one girl and three boys. Maharaj Kumar Bhawani Singh, (Bubbles) was nine, Maharaj Kumar Jai Singh (Joey) was seven and Maharaj Kumar Prithviraj Singh (Pat) was five.

avoided formal receptions in Ooty for fear of offending the elder and more orthodox princes from the other states of India who also happened to be there for the season. In the 1940s no Maharani could show her face in public.

Despite these little restrictions the month that the newly-wed couple spent in Ooty was full of merriment and Gayatri Devi celebrated her twenty-first birthday there.

Thereafter, Maharaja Man Singh left for Bangalore to play polo and join his second wife and the children while the Maharani stayed behind awaiting his letter asking her to join him. When the letter did arrive, the Maharani drove from Ooty to Bangalore, nervous at the

prospect of meeting Second Her Highness. However, her fears were unfounded. Maharaja Man Singh was able to put everybody at ease and made sure that there was no tension between them. In Bangalore, the Maharani also got to spend more time with her husband's four children—Maharaj Kumar Bhawani Singh or Bubbles and Maharaj Kumari Prem Kanwar or Mickey, the children of First Her Highness Maharani Saheb Marudhar Kanwar, and with Maharaj Kumar Jai Singh or Joey and Maharaj Kumar Prithvi Raj Singh or Pat, the two boys of Second Her Highness Maharani Saheb Kishore Kanwar. The entire family stayed in Bangalore for two weeks and then it was time to leave for Jaipur.

A tour of Jaipur State.
Maharaja Man Singh out on a field trip in Jaipur State.

Life in Jaipur

Wisdom is the supreme part
of happiness.

—Sophocles

ayatri Devi had been to Jaipur on several occasions but those were very informal visits with hardly any protocol that she was expected to follow. This trip, however, was different. It was her first trip as the Maharani of Jaipur. A special salon brought the royal couple with their retinue to Viman Bhawan, their own personal waiting rooms at the Jaipur Railway Station.

The Viman Bhawan is still there, but today it is surrounded by a residential colony and houses government settlement offices. It is in a state of disrepair though signs of its original beauty are still visible in the decorative plaster, the insignia and the high ceilings. The rooms where the Maharaja and Maharani once waited to board a train, where they freshened up when they arrived from outside Jaipur, are now peopled by very official looking gentlemen of the government with heaps of files on both sides of their tables. The high ceilings have been reduced to almost half their height, and covered by wooden panels to make them suitable for coolers and air conditioners.

In the past this comfortably furnished suite had two separate wings—the *mardana* and the *zenana*—for the Maharaja and Maharani and their important guests where they could change and freshen up, and appear before the public. It was also more convenient for visiting dignitaries to board the train away from the crowded public station.

Maharaja Sawai Man Singh II.
Mor Mukat Singh who later became Maharaja Sawai Man Singh II, was the younger of the two sons of Sawai Singh, the Thakur of Isarda, a village near Sawai Madhopur. He was adopted by the Maharaja of Jaipur, Madho Singh. When the Maharaja died in 1922, Mor Mukat Singh became the thirty-ninth ruler of the Kachchawa clan at the age of eleven.

FACING PAGE:

At Jaipur.
When Maharani Gayatri Devi arrived in Jaipur after her wedding, it was a spectacular city.

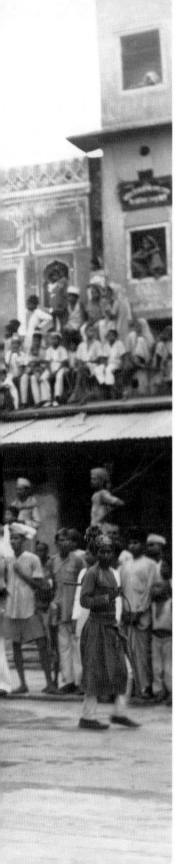

As the train approached Jaipur, Maharaja Man Singh gently told the new Maharani to be prepared to cover her head. When the train rolled into the station, her maids from Cooch Behar were waiting for her with a dressy *paushak*—the traditional Rajasthani costume that she had to wear. The maids of the second Maharani, Kishore Kanwar, were also present at the station to help her don the paushak consisting of a *lehenga* (skirt), *a kurti kanchli* (two-piece blouse) and an *odhna* (sari). Rajmata recalls, ' As a new bride I had to wear a bright red paushak with all the traditional jewellery.'

Maharaja Man Singh's two married sisters received her outside Viman Bhawan and escorted her to Amber. Amber Fort houses the Jaipur family shrine—the Shila Devi Temple. It was a ritual with Maharaja Man Singh that whenever he left the state for any length of time, the first thing he did on his return was to offer prayers at the Shila Devi Temple. Rajmata has tried to maintain the tradition to this day. She also visits the Moti Doongri Ganesh Temple before she leaves the city.

The present condition of Amber Fort pains her, 'I wish somebody would do something about Amber. What have they done to this beautiful monument? There are unauthorized showrooms and hawkers all over the fort. Sometimes I feel like visiting the temple with a blindfold so that I don't have to see all the destruction.'

A ceremonial procession in Jaipur.

Ceremonial processions in Jaipur were eagerly awaited by the general public. People would even climb on to rooftops for a good view of the elephants, camels and mounted guards from the Jaipur State Forces.

Gangaur Puja.

The new Maharani was not fully conversant with the main festivals of Rajasthan such as Gangaur, Teej, Diwali and Holi during which pujas had to be performed by the Maharanis in the zenana of the City Palace. She was fortunate to have the guidance of the two senior Maharanis.

But when she arrived in Jaipur it was a beautiful city with broad streets, palaces and forts and its temples and huge gardens.

Her first home was Rambagh Palace and having come from a lush green countryside she was relieved to see the beautiful gardens surrounding the palace. Rambagh, though thoroughly modern in its design and planning, was built along the traditional pattern of separate wings for the Maharaja—the mardana, and for the Maharani—the zenana. An addition in this new palace was a nursery for the children, and a wing for the various guests who called on the Jaipurs. Maharani Gayatri Devi's wing had been modernized

by Maharaja Man Singh. She was delighted that so much care had gone into doing up her apartments just to her taste.

'His Highness had his rooms specially redecorated for me by his favourite interior designer, Hammonds of London. The rooms had pale cream fitted carpets, light pink walls, beautiful chandeliers and pale pink brocade curtains embellishing the wide windows. My bedroom was the prettiest in the palace, furnished with a bed of soft silk satin with light brocade bedspreads, a colourful divan, two armchairs with silver legs and a mirrored dressing table trimmed with pleated silk satin.'

Life in Jaipur was certainly different from the one she was accustomed to. The grandeur of the City Palace, the court and the formality of the court proceedings took some getting used to. The easy informality and Western lifestyle of Cooch Behar were replaced

TOP:

Durbar.

Jaipur is surrounded by small towns, or thikanas, *each headed by a thakur who owed allegiance to the Maharaja. The thakurs were given special status according to land ownerships or services provided to the Maharaja. At a durbar at the City Palace the thakurs are seated in order of their importance.*

LEFT:

A display of discipline.

The Rajendra Hazari Guards at the City Palace.

A function at the City Palace.

A lot of grand functions were held at the City Palace during the time of Maharaja Man Singh II. Each event was meticulously planned and preparations began months in advance. The sheer grandeur and magnitude of these occasions bedazzled the visiting dignitaries. The Maharaja looked dashing in his full military uniform with the beautiful Maharani by his side.

by the formal and traditional affairs of the state. Rajmata says, 'His Highness never used to say that I couldn't go out, that I couldn't do this or that. But I knew I mustn't be seen in the front portion of Rambagh and all that.'

'Every morning we used to go riding and swimming. But I did observe the purdah when I went for the formal *griha pravesh* ceremony at City Palace and on other formal occasions.'

The first ten days after her arrival in Jaipur were a succession of religious ceremonies and formal get-togethers where she met all the relatives and close friends of Maharaja Man Singh.

After marriage she didn't take too long to adapt to this new lifestyle. 'During the war years, many officers were recalled to duty and I was asked to take over the running of the household. Guests, including several Maharajas and polo players during the season,

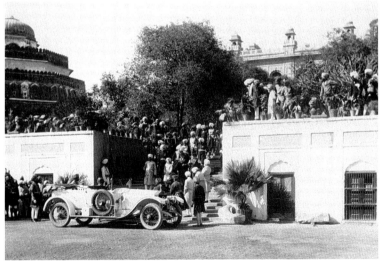

TOP AND LEFT:

Receiving dignitaries.

The City Palace figured prominently on the itinerary of every visiting dignitary from abroad or other princely states of India. Each such visitor was given a befitting ceremonial welcome, and as a state guest lived in the City Palace. The Maharani would personally supervise the arrangements for the guests.

TOP:

Dining room, Lilypool.

MIDDLE AND BOTTOM:

Sitting room, Lilypool.

FACING PAGE:

Sheesh Mahal, City Palace

The gold and mirror work at the Shobha Niwas or Sheesh Mahal reflects the baroque opulence of the Rajasthani style. This is one of the most beautiful sections of the City Palace, used mainly as a sitting room where guests were required to take off their shoes before entering, and sit on mattresses on the floor.

Queen Elizabeth and Prince Philip.

When Queen Elizabeth and Prince Philip visited Jaipur in 1961 on Maharaja Man Singh's invitation it meant several months of planning. Officials from Buckingham Palace and the British Foreign Office were in touch with the Protocol Division in Delhi months ahead of the trip. On the occasion, the Jaipurs, held a spectacular durbar in her honour at the City Palace.

BELOW:

Arriving in style.

Queen Elizabeth was escorted to the City Palace on a richly caparisoned elephant.

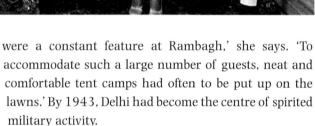

were a constant feature at Rambagh,' she says. 'To accommodate such a large number of guests, neat and comfortable tent camps had often to be put up on the lawns.' By 1943, Delhi had become the centre of spirited military activity.

The Viceroy and Vicereine, Lord and Lady Mountbatten were amongst the many political dignitaries from all over the world who had to be received and feted. Presidents, prime ministers, ambassadors, royal personages from other countries and sometimes friends were received at the Rambagh and taken for shikar camps to Ranthambhore (now a

national tiger sanctuary) in Sawai Madhopur. And the guests looked forward to these hunting trips.

Rajmata still has close ties with Ranthambhore. She is a patron of the World Wildlife Fund and takes keen interest in their activities. Her long-standing interest in the preservation of wildlife sees her visiting her once favourite hunting ground, Ranthambhore, as often as she can, and not just for a holiday. She has been instrumental in getting huge funding from overseas for the relocation of villages that fall within the sanctuary. Every time she is in Sawai Madhopur she likes to visit these villages and see the progress for herself. That is not an easy task because the roads leading to some of these villages are not even properly laid. Her staff members accompanying her on

Fancy dress at Lilypool with the Maharaj Kumar of Baria.

At a fancy dress party at Lilypool, the Maharani relaxes with her son-in-law, the Maharaj Kumar of Baria, who married Maharaja Man Singh's only daughter and eldest child, Prem Kumari, better known as Mickey.

these trips are more concerned about how she would be able to handle the strain. She is not worried about the bumpy jeep rides as long as she can ensure that the money is being properly utilized. She is genuinely concerned about the well-being of the villagers and spends her evenings in Sawai Madhopur listening to their problems and providing help whenever possible.

With the Mountbattens.

At the Silver Jubilee of Maharaja Man Singh's accession to the throne in 1947.

TOP:

A warm welcome.

The Mountbattens welcomed at the Jaipur airport by the Jaipurs.

Soon after marriage however, the new Maharani was something of a novelty for the staid and traditional city of Jaipur and not everyone was happy to welcome this modern Maharani who moved around freely and accompanied the Maharaja to parties. There was resistance from most of the nobles who had been used to keeping their womenfolk at home.

Despite these minor problems, life became more and more interesting as the days went by. When Maharaja Man Singh told her that he wanted her to try and get the women out of the purdah, she took it upon herself as a challenge. She said to him, 'Give me a school and I'll do it.'

In 1943, just after three years of marriage, she started a school for Rajput women. Maharaja Man Singh enlisted the help of the knowledgeable and enlightened Pandit Amarnath Atal, the Finance Minister; Sir Mirza Ismail, the Dewan of Jaipur State; Savitri Bharatiya, the Inspectress of Schools and a few other progressive people. Very soon a suitable building, Madho Vilas, was located and word was sent around that girls should be prepared to enroll in the school.

Knowing the Maharani's passion for the unconventional, the nobles were quite prepared for these revolutionary schemes. There was a bit of resistance but most people thought it was one of those passing fancies that would die a natural death; it would be easier to go along with the idea rather than oppose it.

'Why do I consider education so important?' explains Rajmata. 'Well, I was fortunate enough to receive a sound education and had very enlightened, strong women on my mother's side of the family. I

The First Lady of America.

Jacqueline Kennedy and Maharaja Man Singh at a picnic.

A family friend.

Jacqueline Kennedy, wife of the American President John F. Kennedy, was a close friend of the Jaipurs. She came to Jaipur on a semi-official tour soon after the Maharani had won the elections with a huge majority. The Government of Rajasthan was not too pleased with this visit and thought of it more as the royal family's ploy to gain political mileage out of it.

realized that if I wanted to draw women out of the purdah then I would have to do a lot more than organize tournaments, raffles and parties at the Ladies Club. Fortunately His Highness agreed with me and I was able to start the Maharani Gayatri Devi Girls School,' says Rajmata. It went on to become the first public school for girls in Asia.

A report published in the *Civil & Military Gazette, Lahore, India* on 1 February 1936 highlighted her grandmother the Maharani of Baroda's views on educating women, in her presidential address at the fourth session of the National Council of Women in Calcutta. She had said: 'There is much scope for reform in the education of our daughters and it is our duty to see that they are given that training which will fit them to play their part in national affairs and at the same time make them more efficient mothers. One

TOP AND BOTTOM:

Shikar at Sawai Madhopur.

Sawai Madhopur, about 180 km southeast of Jaipur, was an area that both the Maharaja and the Maharani loved. Their big-game shoots were well known and their guests eagerly awaited the day. A totally separate section in the Palace was in charge of organizing these shooting camps, and left for Sawai Madhopur weeks in advance to ensure that these camps went off smoothly.

of the best things that we could do for our country would be to
establish schools in which accent was laid on social qualities; schools
in which the knowledge which the pupils acquired would be a really
formative influence in their lives; a knowledge of themselves and of
their duty to their fellows which would help them to realize
themselves fully as women, and not lead them to think themselves
superior simply because they were labelled Bachelors of Art.'

Ready for the shikar.

*The Maharani played the perfect
hostess to her guests during a
shooting camp, and never let up a
chance of bagging a good game
herself.*

71

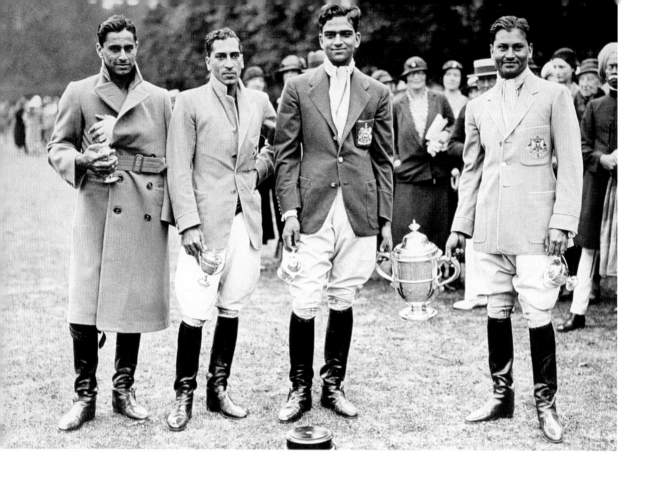

The Jaipur Polo Team.

The Jaipur Polo Team won all the tournaments when it went abroad in 1933. From left to right: Maharaja Prithvi Singh of Baria, Rao Raja Abhay Singh, Maharaja Man Singh of Jaipur and Rao Raja Hanut Singh.

The influence of her mother and her Baroda grandmother, Maharani Chimnabai, was very strong indeed and on 3 July 1943, Pandit Amarnath Atal and several prominent citizens assembled at Madho Vilas to declare open the Maharani Gayatri Devi Girls Public School. Forty young, hesitant and nervous girls, of varying age groups and six teachers were present in that gathering. The girls were overawed by the fact that they had been brought to this building away from their dolls and their retinue of maids. Prafulla Kumari, a businesswoman now in her sixties, was one of the students on that day. 'I didn't really understand what was going on. My mother had asked the maid to make sure that I was dressed on time to leave for Maharani Sahib's new school. All I remember of that day is being given *patashas* and handkerchiefs. I went to Madho Vilas for one year and in July 1944, the new school building was ready so we moved there.'

The prospectus of the school in 1943 stated: 'The aims of the institution will be... To secure to the pupils the advantages of training in home craft and domestic hygiene, for the betterment and happiness of their homes, to create in them a taste for fine arts, colour decoration and culture...to create, through games, good physique an *esprit de corps* in the girls. In general, the aim and effort would be, to impart an all-round education to the girls, which will prepare them to play the role required of them, as efficient members of the society.'

Rajput nobility and later women from the middle class continued to join the school and within a few years the students increased in number to several hundreds. It wasn't long before the school became a national institution. For the women of Rajasthan, Maharani Gayatri Devi's single most important contribution to the state has been her role in the emancipation of women through education.

Rajmata, however, is loath to taking all the credit for this. 'Miss L.G. Lutter played a very important role in taking the school to such great heights. She was a dedicated Principal and had to plan different activities for the varying age groups that we had,' says Rajmata.

Students of this prestigious school later went on to join the IFS, IAS; they became doctors, engineers, writers, scientists and educationists. Maharani Gayatri Devi herself set an example: she wore trousers, drove her car, played tennis and went horseback riding. She was an icon for women throughout the country. Girls from very orthodox families, where the womenfolk rarely went to school, and were educated enough only to be able to sign their names and read simple letters, were now proudly encouraging their daughters to study so that they could take their rightful place in society. My purdah-clad mother, influenced no doubt by the beautiful Maharani, was happy to let me pursue a career in writing.

Jagat Singh Mehta, former foreign secretary and husband of the late writer Rama Mehta, is fulsome in his praise of Rajmata: 'She doesn't realize it but she was a revolutionary. She was an educationist who started this school for girls and made it possible for women all

Receiving a trophy.

Often, the Maharani gave the winners' trophy away to the Jaipur Polo Team. As captain of the Jaipur Polo Team, it was invariably the Maharaja himself who accepted the trophy.

Maharani Gayatri Devi Girls School.

The MGD School continued to grow under her guidance and that of the principal, Miss L.G. Lutter. The Maharani visited the school regularly to see the progress that students were making. She always had a word of encouragement for everyone, and the students just loved to have her in their midst

over Rajasthan to come out of the purdah. She was the first woman to attend a public function in Udaipur in 1952 and that caused quite a stir. One young Muslim boy known to me remembers that his traditional burqa-clad mother also attended that function in a sari, with her head uncovered.'

The forties and fifties saw Maharani Gayatri Devi in her role as an educationist and a social reformer but the world at large was more attracted to a totally different side of her personality: her beauty.

She was a natural beauty (interestingly, she hardly ever uses any make up on her face!) and a large part of her elegance also came from the fact that she was intelligent and had a deep commitment to social

issues. Rajmata had followed, until a few years ago, a very strict regimen of yoga, tennis, swimming and riding. Her knees have started giving her a bit of a problem these days but that hasn't stopped her from visiting family and friends and travelling extensively. Sometimes, it is difficult to keep pace with her. Her young ADC, Hanuwant Singh, is very impressed by her active schedule, 'She is so energetic that we get a complex being around with her! She often says to me that if she lets herself think about her aches and pains then that'll be the beginning of the end. She would just take to bed.'

David Barwara, son of Rabbit Barwara, a very close friend of Maharaja Man Singh, was only seven years old when he first saw

Out of the purdah.

Students who joined the school in the late forties and fifties came from orthodox backgrounds, and had never been encouraged to dance. The attractive Maharani introduced dancing classes in school and encouraged the students to perform on stage. She would often drop in to see them during practice sessions.

Rajmata. He later became a close friend of Maharaj Jagat Singh, Rajmata's only son, and spent a lot of time with him. Says he of her with a whiff of nostalgia, 'She has always looked stunning but I remember one time when she came for a party to Barwara House. She arrived in a red sports car, a two-seater with an open hood that she was driving herself, dressed in a red sari. I still remember that day so clearly. I don't think I'll ever see a woman more beautiful than her in this lifetime.'

The famous photographer Cecil Beaton named her one of the ten most beautiful women in the world.

The Grande Dame of Romance, the late Barbara Cartland noted in her book *Beauty and Health:* 'Ayesha Jaipur has been called the loveliest woman in the world. She is, when one sees her, breathtakingly beautiful with that fascinating feminine grace which is characteristic of Indian women. She has also an excellent brain and a capacity for hard work. She has for ten years represented Jaipur in Parliament. Jaipur with its pink palaces full of incredible treasures, tiger-infested green hills, marble rocks and atmosphere of mystery, is a fitting background for someone so exquisite that a poet wrote of her:"Her face is lovelier than the golden light, Which brings the Indian dawn..."

'Ayesha Jaipur has friends all over the world, from the poor families she

'Her eyes mirror her soul.'

Cecil Beaton, the famous photographer had named the Maharani as one of the ten most beautiful women in the world. It was an opinion shared by many.

FACING PAGE:

In each other's arms.

The royal couple waltzing at a party.

represents in India who look on her as their champion and protector, to the royal and social figures of the West . . .

'She has a deep compassion for the suffering, but also a strong desire to do something to help. She is one of those rare people of whom one can truthfully say: "Her eyes mirror her soul."'

Getting to Know the Family

*To know the road ahead,
ask those coming back.*

—Chinese proverb

Rajmata's relationship with Maharaja Man Singh's family had its fair share of ups and downs but on the whole progressed rather smoothly. Things were never allowed to come to a head because Maharaja Man Singh was very strict in this matter and did not approve of any kind of loose talk. He ensured that his staff and others did not play one Maharani against the other and was quick to show his displeasure if any untoward incident was brought to his notice.

Maharaja Man Singh was very fond of his first two wives even though these were arranged marriages. He tried to spend as much time with them as possible. Maharani Marudhar Kanwar, First Her Highness spent quite a lot of time in Jodhpur, her parental home. She was conservative in her upbringing and had simple tastes; she kept to her own section of the palace and did not interfere in the day-to-day lives of the other family members. She was given the respect and importance due to her and conducted all traditional and religious ceremonies. There was no question of Maharani Gayatri Devi taking precedence over the other two wives in these matters. Maharani Kishore Kanwar, 'Jo Didi', was more modern in her outlook and had the task of running the zenana in the City Palace.

FACING PAGE:

Life at the City Palace.

The young Maharani was quick to adapt to the demands of her new and rather traditional set-up in Jaipur, despite hailing from the Westernized and liberal Cooch Behar family.

79

Jo Didi.

On 31 December 1921 when Maharaja Man Singh was just ten years old, he was formally betrothed to Marudhar Kanwar, the twenty-two-year-old sister of Maharaja Umaid Singh of Jodhpur, as well as to Kishore Kanwar, the daughter of his younger brother Maharaja Sumer Singh. Both aunt and niece became the First and Second Maharanis of Jaipur. Man Singh called Maharani Kishore Kanwar 'Jo', short for Jodhpur, her home state. She became Jo Didi to Gayatri Devi.

FACING PAGE:

Dancing the ghoomar.

The beautiful Maharani performs the traditional Rajasthani dance, ghoomar, with her guests.

She was the one who made all the necessary arrangements on festive occasions and controlled the state jewellery. Each of the Maharanis had her own place in Maharaja Man Singh's life but it was understood that his third wife, the one that he had chosen himself, was his official hostess and accompanied him whenever he travelled. First Her Highness died in 1944 after battling a liver ailment for several years. Second Her Highness died many years later in 1958 due to a gall bladder ailment.

Initially the new Maharani did meet with a bit of resistance. She was seen as an eastern princess with no knowledge of Rajput traditions and customs. Nobody, however, dared to voice his or her concerns. Maharaja Man Singh's sister Chand Baisa, Rajmata Sahiba of Katiyari, gives all the credit for this to her brother: '*Darbar* (His Highness) did not approve of anyone insulting any of the Maharanis. People were afraid of voicing any negative feelings towards his third marriage for fear of making Darbar angry. There was also the fear of having their jagirs confiscated. He did not like anyone interfering in his personal matters and people were expected to mind their own business and hold their tongue.' A joke doing the rounds those days was that whenever the young Maharani drove past in her car, the orthodox Rajputs would say, 'Let's turn our faces away or else go indoors. We'll have to maintain the purdah since our new Maharani Sahib will not.'

If this attitude bothered Maharani Gayatri Devi she chose not to show it, nor did she let it trouble her too much. She was an independent woman who enjoyed her husband's support. She was also fortunate to have the support of the two older Maharanis and shared a cordial relationship with them.

'We gave First Her Highness the respect that was due to her as she was the senior most Maharani of Jaipur. But as she was older and didn't really travel too much I had more interaction with Second Her Highness. She went to England twice a year with His Highness and when she was in India we travelled together on many occasions. She was always there to guide me and she taught me a lot of things about

A day at the Rajmahal Palace.

Days at the Rajmahal Palace were quite hectic. There were guests to be entertained, parties to be organized, election meetings to be held. And then there was the Maharaja's favourite Alsatian to play with.

the customs here, how to welcome people, how to greet them and so on. I remember when I was coming to Jaipur from Bangalore for the first time after marriage it was Second Her Highness who told me that there would be *Gangaur* puja when I reached. And as I didn't know how to go about it she demonstrated everything for me and made sure that I knew exactly what to do and when. I was relieved and just followed her instructions in such matters. She was an attractive person, very neat and meticulous in everything that she did—in the way she dressed and in the way she worked. Everything had to be perfect. His Highness had always told me that she would take precedence over me and I always respected that.

'I know there was a lot of resentment but the one redeeming factor was that it rained the day I arrived so the people of Jaipur blessed the new bride for the rain!'

A little restriction here and there didn't stop her from doing the things she liked doing—playing tennis, horseback riding, partying, going for picnics and shikars, encouraging women to step out of the confines of their homes. An endearing aspect of her nature was her sense of humour and her love for playing practical jokes on her guests. Chand Baisa recalls an incident that took place in the late fifties.

'One day we had nothing to do and were getting bored so Maharani Sahib (Gayatri Devi) decided to visit some friends. I happily agreed until I realized that she wanted to go in a bullock cart! I was horrified and very worried that His Highness would get annoyed with me for allowing her to do so. I tried my best to dissuade her but she can be quite stubborn. So here we were, the two of us, in some poor man's covered bullock cart that was carrying hay. He was too scared to protest so he took us to this house and went right up to the porch. The lady of the house came out shouting and abusing the poor man for bringing the cart into the house without permission. The poor man could only mumble that the "passengers" had forced him to come right up till here. Unable to control her laughter anymore, Maharani Sahib coolly jumped down from the cart. After the lady recovered from her shock she begged the Maharani not to

play such pranks again otherwise His Highness would throw them out of the state!

She was so full of fun and games that there was never a dull moment when she was around.'

Friends and relatives visited her regularly and parties and picnics were organized to entertain them. The shikar camps and cooking parties of those times are remembered fondly to this day.

Chand Baisa also remembers a 'skeleton party': 'His Highness was away in the Middle East and come evening the ladies would start getting a little bored. One evening Maharani Sahib said to us, "Let's

With Vivien Leigh, Bubbles, Joey.

Bubbles and Joey look on as the Maharani chats with actress Vivien Leigh. The children travelled extensively with the Maharani, and met all kinds of interesting people wherever they went.

have a skeleton party!" First Her Highness said, "My happiness lies in seeing you all happy so do what you want to do." Only a few of us were in on the secret. So it was decided that there would be a dinner at Lilypool (Rajmata's present residence) and somebody would be made to wear black clothes with a skeleton drawn on it. This "skeleton" would be lowered slowly from the terrace with the help of a rope. The entire garden area would be in darkness and just the area where the "skeleton" was to be lowered would be lit up enough for the "skeleton" to show. Maharani Sahib said, "We'll see how many people get scared and how many are really

brave." When the "skeleton" was lowered there was chaos because most of the guests were so scared that they didn't even stay long enough to have dinner! It was a crazy scene with some people saying their prayers and some insisting that *Mataji* had come to give them darshan! So you see that is the kind of mischievous person she was.'

These practical jokes were normal in the zenana, or the ladies section of the Rambagh, but this section was a very tame version of the original zenana of the City Palace during Maharaja Madho Singh's time. It is believed that he had nine wives, 7000 concubines and several children. Rajmata remembers that when she came to Jaipur in 1940 there were some 400 women still living there, 'They were widowed relatives and their daughters as well as servants and attendants; the Dowager Maharani and her retinue of ladies-in-waiting, maids, cooks, and other servants. All the retainers of the late Maharaja's other wives could not be dismissed just because their mistresses had died, and so they remained the responsibility of the ruling family.'

When Maharani Gayatri Devi came to Jaipur the zenana was bustling with activity. Each of the three Maharanis had her self-contained apartments with several maids and *nadars* (eunuchs) on

Holi at the City Palace.

Holi was a much-awaited festival celebrated in the City Palace gardens in the traditional way. Natural colours were used and guests were served sweets and drinks. The revelry continued well into dusk.

FACING PAGE:
The beautiful prankster.

Maharani Gayatri Devi loved to play pranks in the zenana. Once, she organized a 'skeleton' party to scare away guests whom she had invited for dinner.

duty. Each of these apartments had a durbar hall where the womenfolk held special *mehfils* (soirées) to mark the religious functions and festivals, and gathered together on other occasions like birthdays, engagements, marriages and childbirth. So complete was their world here that these women hardly ever needed to go out or interact with outsiders.

In keeping with tradition, one section of the zenana was given exclusively to the third Maharani and that became her own domain where she was free to entertain, hold pujas and meet with Rajput ladies of the *thikanas* (nobility).

'All the apartments were almost identical. Mine was painted in blues and greens and like the others it had a little square courtyard and a private durbar with blue glass lamps, and several smaller rooms opening off it. I came to know the area better as we had to go there on all ceremonial occasions. We sometimes stayed on for as long as a fortnight,' recalls Rajmata.

The zenana of the City Palace is in shambles today with unkempt and deserted *rawalas* (apartments). The beautifully painted walls are a shadow of their original beauty. The plaster on the walls is chipping off. Old *bahi-khatas* (books and notebooks) stacked in dingy rooms have been shredded by white ants. Wild vegetation has overrun the once decorated walls, and the gardens where mehfils were held have been reduced to dry, weed-infested ruins.

Rajmata still visits her rawala and is saddened by its condition.

'There was an agreement wherein the maintenance of the zenana was taken over by the State Government. But it has really been neglected all these years. I hope they can put it to some appropriate use. There used to be so much activity and so much life here...' She has written several times to the State Government reminding them of their responsibility.

On her birthday every year, ever since she came to Jaipur, she has been holding a durbar in the zenana where a puja is held for her health and longevity. It is customary for the women who are invited to come dressed in heavy embroidered paushaks and offer a token of

At an official dinner.

The Jaipurs at one of the many parties they attended on their trips abroad.

At a puja.

Despite his Western education, Maharaja Man Singh II never moved too far away from his traditional upbringing. All religious occasions were marked by a puja held in the palace. Here he is seen with pundits during a puja.

Presenting the nazar.

Maharaja Man Singh II at the City Palace Durbar Hall during a durbar. A man presents a token or nazar *to mark his obeisance to the Maharaja.*

their obeisance and do the traditional *ghoomar* dance in her honour. Refreshments are also organized on these occasions.

In her early years in Jaipur there was never a dull moment. She revived the various social and sporting activities of the Ladies Club. Being a good badminton and tennis player herself, she soon went on to become the President of both the Badminton and Tennis Associations. She enjoyed her game of tennis and ended up playing mainly with male partners because hardly any woman could play the game. She played golf and went riding as well.

Mrs Savitri Bharatiya, an educationist and later the Principal of a local women's college, wrote a very interesting article on the Rajmata in a local paper: 'The new Maharani was doing unimaginable things: she had started going to the kitchen and supervising it, she was on the fields playing badminton and tennis,

she had bobbed her hair, wore slacks, drove the car, watched polo, and could be seen riding, not only in the Rambagh Palace grounds but also on the roads alongside the Maharaja. Maharani Gayatri Devi started exploring possibilities and as a first step she started visiting the Ladies Club and meeting on common ground ladies from all walks of life. Her example was soon emulated and, through her personal efforts and persuasion, the *asurya sparshas*—the purdah-ridden—condescended to come into the light of day. The blue-blooded Rajput ladies, the high-browed and commoners alike, started

89

patronizing the Ladies Club... Very soon the Ladies Club became the hub of hectic activities and under its aegis, games, sports, socials, cultural activities and fetes were organized in which all participated with equal gusto.'

A very old member of her staff, Pratap Singh, recalls the time when she had gone to a hotel in Delhi to drop somebody. The *darban* (attendant) opened the car door for her not realizing that she was not getting down. Consequently her hand was painfully pulled with the door. The poor man received a royal firing and she called him a bloody fool.

Once back home, she kept thinking about the incident and asked Pratap Singh if he thought that the darban was upset about the whole thing. Pratap Singh assured her that the darban might well have been quite used to it. She, however, could not get the incident out of her mind and within an hour drove back to the hotel, called the nervous man out and apologized to him explaining that she had not meant to shout at him but had lost her temper because her arm had been hurt.

The poor man was too embarrassed to say anything more than '*Huzur* (Your Highness), what are you doing? Why are you saying sorry? It is all right.' 'How many people would do that?' asks the seventy-five-year-old Pratap Singh, with a lot of admiration in his voice.

The Changing Political Scenario

Nearly all men can stand adversity,
but if you want to test a man's
character, give him power.

—Abraham Lincoln

I n the late 1930s when it became inevitable that India would soon break free from the British Raj, the princes began to wonder about their role in the new politicized India. The new crop of politicians took potshots at the princes and made them out to be undemocratic and merely a creation of the British.

The British Raj was coming to an end and the new government was in no mood to let the rulers continue to enjoy the privileges that they'd had for generations. Their options narrowed, they would be compelled to join the mainstream of life. What followed was resistance and resentment. The princes were not about to give up without a fight. The Chamber of Princes, set up in 1921, had regular meetings and various options were discussed. There was even talk of keeping their states independent of free India. They wondered if they wouldn't be better off forming an entirely separate federation composed only of princely states that could be classified into three categories: Salute States of which there were 118 in all; 117 Non-Salute states, and those run by a few hundred minor princelings.

Despite hectic negotiations and meetings, the princes realized that they were fighting a losing battle. To add to their woes there

Stepping into politics.

Inspired by the political charter
of Chakravarti Rajagopalachari's
Swatantra Party, the Maharani
decided to join politics.

FACING PAGE:

Beyond life in the palace.

Having lead a life of opulence,
the Maharani wanted to give
something back to the people
of Jaipur State.

Chakravarti Rajagopalachari, or Rajaji, founded the Swatantra Party and had many supporters and followers. The young Maharani was one of them. She was, without doubt their party's star attraction at meetings and held Rajaji in high esteem

seemed to be no unity amongst the princes—each one, while being a part of the Chamber of Princes, was also trying to negotiate with the government to get a better deal for himself. The last straw came when the Maharaja of Bikaner walked out of the States Negotiations Committee, set up in 1946, with the appeal that the princes should work towards a united India. That ended all possibility of a separate princely India.

Life had to go on despite all the stress and strife. In 1947, there was a display of princely grandeur. Princess Prem Kumari— Mickey,

94

Maharaja Man Singh's daughter was married to the Maharaj Kumar of Baria.

Rajmata recalls that marriage. 'She was the first Jaipur princess to be married in a hundred years. The wedding and the attendant processions, banquet and celebrations were on a scale of unparalleled lavishness. Everything was arranged meticulously and all traditions and customs were followed. It was perhaps one of the final grand displays of pageantry in princely India.' All the three Maharanis participated, each one giving a *binola* (banquet) for the

For the Founder of Jaipur.

The statue of Maharaja Sawai Jai Singh, the Founder of Jaipur City, was installed in an area later known as Statue Circle. President Zakir Hussain was present on the occasion. Maharaja Man Singh, Maharani Gayatri Devi and Maharaj Kumar Bhawani Singh attended the ceremony.

The people's Maharani.

Maharani Gayatri Devi reassures the people of Jaipur and promises to do all she can for them.

FACING PAGE:

Cradling the new-born.

Maharani Gayatri Devi holds her new-born child in her arms while Maharaja Man Singh looks at his fourth son lovingly.

princess. The famous photographer Henri Cartier-Bresson was in town and took photographs of this marriage later mentioned in *The Guinness Book of World Records* as the most expensive wedding in the world.

This was followed by another magnificent event. Four months after Independence, Maharaja Man Singh held what was to be the last grand function as the Maharaja of Jaipur. In December 1947 he celebrated his Silver Jubilee as the ruler of Jaipur. It was a spectacular affair in which almost the entire city was involved. It also proved, beyond doubt, the great love and affection that the people of Jaipur had for their Maharaja. The culmination of the festivities was a majestic durbar attended by ruling princes from neighbouring states as well as guests like Lord and Lady Mountbatten.

Jagat, her only child.

Jagat was an affectionate child who was very close to his parents. The Maharani believes that he never really got over his father's death.

Meanwhile, amidst the continuing political upheaval the merger of the states became a foregone conclusion. As a result, a lot of changes were forced on the maharajas all over the country. They did continue to receive privy purses and hold their titles of maharajas but the political atmosphere did not hold out any hope for them. The ruling princes were left to negotiate individually with the government for a better deal.

Unfortunately the princes proved to be their own worst enemies. Their extravagant lifestyle and over-indulgent behaviour made it so much easier for the powers that be to bear down on them.

Jaipur was integrated into the new Union of Greater Rajasthan. It was decided that Maharaja Man Singh would be made the Rajpramukh, or hereditary Governor, of Greater Rajasthan. After accepting this Maharaja Man Singh had to hand over all official buildings to the State Government. The property that passed into the hands of the State Government was worth over fifteen million pounds in those days.

Maharaja Man Singh was perhaps one of the very few far-sighted rulers who appreciated that changes were inevitable and was not unduly disturbed by what was to follow. It may be interesting to note that he was also the only ruler whose three sons all held jobs. He took his new role as Rajpramukh very seriously and tried to keep himself occupied doing his duty by his people.

'He had excellent qualities of the head and heart. This enabled him to give the correct lead and guidance to his Cabinet and other administrators in the State of Jaipur. He was a capable statesman and Rajpramukh of Rajasthan. With his perfect tact, disarming smile and great powers of leadership, he always carried his Cabinet forward with him,' observed one of his staff members.

The Maharani stood by her husband Maharaja Man Singh during these difficult times. In October 1949, the year in which Maharaja Man Singh became Rajpramukh, she gave birth to her only child, a son who was named Jagat.

It was a normal childbirth and she spent one month in Bombay

where Jagat was born. 'Although Jaipur was no longer a princely state, the Chief Minister of Rajasthan declared a public holiday and cannons were fired to commemorate the birth of the baby boy. People from all over the state came to Rambagh to congratulate the Maharaja, likening him to King Dashratha of the epic *Ramayana*, who also had four sons.'

This sense of well-being, however, did not last too long. In October 1956, Maharaja Man Singh received letters from the President of India Dr Rajendra Prasad, the Prime Minister Pandit Jawaharlal Nehru and the Home Minister Shri Govind Vallabh Pant

Picnic in England.

This family portrait of the Maharaja and Maharani with the four sons, Bubbles, Joey, Pat and Jagat, was taken in London.

99

A crowd -puller.

*During her election campaigns,
people turned out in large
numbers to listen to her and also
air their grievances.*

informing him that he would cease to be Rajpramukh from 31 October 1956. Although this was as unexpected as it was abrupt, it didn't really surprise Maharaja Man Singh but for the shoddy manner in which the matter had been handled.

He brought about some more changes in his lifestyle. He became a pioneer when he turned Rambagh Palace into a hotel and moved his family to Rajmahal Palace. This action drew a lot of criticism from the other princes but it was a revolutionary step later emulated by almost every maharaja in Rajasthan. 'Bubbles and I were in Delhi when we heard about his decision and we said, "How could you do this?" He said, "We don't need a palace but Jaipur needs a hotel." He was a very modern and progressive ruler and moved with the times. He did not stand on ceremony and had his feet firmly planted to the ground,' says Rajmata of her late husband.

Life continued under these changed circumstances and there were important guests who had to be entertained, like Queen Elizabeth II who arrived in 1961, followed by other dignitaries like Jacqueline Kennedy.

Maharani Gayatri Devi watched her husband's fluctuating fortunes but there was little that she could do to ease his tension. The Chief Minister of Rajasthan met her and asked her to join the Congress Party and be their candidate from Jaipur but she refused. Rajmata says, 'I was getting more and more fed up of the Congress government.' So were a lot of other people. Chakravarti Rajagopalachari (Rajaji), a much respected elder statesman of India, who had been one of Mahatma Gandhi's closest associates had left the party because he did not agree with some of Prime Minister Nehru's policies, especially the one on co-operative farming.

When Rajaji decided to form the Swatantra Party he found many followers who had begun to grow a little disgruntled with the Congress, the then ruling party.

The Maharani herself had never seriously thought of being a part of any political party so her decision to join the Swatantra Party was neither well-planned nor well thought out, even though she had

been toying with the idea for a long time. She remembers, 'Though His Highness and I were both attracted to the veteran leader C. Rajagopalachari's newly formed opposition party the Swatantra Party, His Highness felt disinclined to enter party politics. One morning I just asked him if I could join the Party and he said "Yes." As I was leaving for my morning ride I asked the ADC to invite the local secretary of the Swatantra Party over for breakfast. When I returned, the man was waiting for me and I inquired how one went about joining a political party. I found that it was a very simple process of filling a form and paying a subscription fees. Both my son Pat and I joined the Party.'

She did not think that the Congress, which was also the ruling

Jagat with a pet.

Jagat loved dogs and spent a lot of time playing with them on the lawns of Rambagh Palace.

101

Love and respect.

When the Maharani was out campaigning, people received her with respect and warmth. She always gave her husband Maharaja Man Singh credit for their warmth because they really loved him.

party, would view this step as an act of defiance and that this decision of hers would cause a lot of bad feeling within the government. And the government did not know of her decision to join the Opposition until Rajaji came to Jaipur. All manner of letters were exchanged between the State and Central Government's leaders and efforts were made to persuade the Maharani to join the Congress Party. It was a case of bad timing as this happened just a few days before the arrival of the Queen. The government dithered over the official programme of the Queen—could there be a reception at the City Palace for the Queen? Was it politically correct for Her Majesty to attend such a function? In the end, however, the Queen did visit the Jaipurs, her good friends, and attended the glittering reception held in her honour at the City Palace.

As a politician Maharani Gayatri Devi was an astounding success. In her first election in 1962 she won by a margin of 3,50,000 votes, the highest ever in the world as noted by *The Guinness Book of World Records*. Later President John F. Kennedy spoke about her as 'the woman with the most staggering majority that anyone has ever earned in an election.'

After the elections the Jaipur royal family was in Delhi in full strength. Maharaja Man Singh was nominated as a member to the Rajya Sabha while Maharaj Jai Singh won his seat from Malpura and Maharaj Prithvi Raj from Dausa. If people expected her to be nervous and stumble over her maiden speech they were disappointed because she was confident and spoke forcefully.

'Of course, I was nervous,' she says now. 'Only I didn't want to

With the masses.

Elections also meant meeting a cross section of people on a fairly regular basis. Sometimes the meetings were held in her own office and at times out in the villages. Party workers, campaigners and her own team of workers toiled with her sincerely, determined to ensure her victory at the polls.

The Maharaja of Jaipur in England.

show it. However, once I started speaking, everything just turned out right.'

The one positive thing about politics was that it took her to many parts of the country as well as to the interiors of Rajasthan. She met people all over the countryside sharing meals with them and speaking to them about their problems and fears. Respectfully called 'Maharani sa' she brought glamour to the staid world of politics. Her election meetings were always well attended. The tremendous popularity of Maharaja Man Singh also contributed to a large extent. She made an impact wherever she went.

'I still remember the last election speech very distinctly in which His Highness addressed the huge crowd as '*tu*' and I was worried that they may resent it. But obviously he was following the traditional relationship of a father addressing his children. He said, "We have built up many generations of affection. The new government has taken my state from me, but for all I care they can take the shirt off my back as long as I can keep that bond of trust and affection between you and me. They accuse me of putting up my wife and two of my sons for election. They say that if I had a hundred and seventy-six sons (the number of seats in the Rajasthan Assembly) I would put them all up too. But they don't know, do they, that I have far more than only one hundred and seventy-six sons?" The response from the crowds was astounding and I knew without doubt that I would win the elections.'

Raj Rana Hari Singh Tana, an eyewitness at one of her election campaigns in Jaipur recalls, 'Pandit Nehru addressed one meeting in Jaipur and said "Maharani Sahib is like a daughter to me. If she were so keen to enter politics she should have come to us, we would have welcomed her."' Later there was another meeting at Badi Chaupar in Jaipur this time addressed by Indira Gandhi. The anger in her voice was quite obvious. She said, '*Aurat kaisi hoti hai? Jo parliament main aati hai janta ki sewa karne woh aurat aise kanch ki gudiya ke tarah nahin hoti jo dusron ka likha hua padh kar suna de.*' (Is this how a woman should be? She should come to Parliament to serve people and not be like a glass doll who just reads what somebody else has written for her.)

India was going through troubled times in the early sixties. China had invaded India in 1962. Pandit Nehru died in 1964 and Lal Bahadur Shastri became the Prime Minister of the country.

In 1965, a few years after Maharani Gayatri Devi became a politician, Maharaja Man Singh was invited to become the Ambassador to Spain. He spent two years there. This was a clever political move by the government because the then Chief Minister Mohan Lal Sukhadia had earlier conveyed his concern to Prime Minister Lal Bahadur Shastri that if the Jaipur royal family continued to be actively involved in politics then the Congress Party would lose its stronghold in Rajasthan.

The stylish Maharaja and his beautiful Maharani were the toast of Madrid. They entertained and threw the most talked about parties in Spain. Maharani Gayatri Devi found Spain quite interesting and noted in her diary a few days after her birthday in 1967: 'I must say they talk very loudly and very fast in Spain. It used to drive me crazy when I was in the department store struggling to explain what I wanted. There was a loud speaker blaring all the time. At the hairdresser's too this constant and loud rapid chatter got on one's nerves. But by and large I love Spain. The people are friendly and life is leisurely—one never seems to be in a hurry. For someone like me who always wants to do something it is astounding how people just sit around and talk!'

They travelled all over Europe and were feted as the most beautiful couple in the society papers. In

The Maharani being received by government officials at a state function in Delhi.

105

In Cannes on the silver wedding anniversary.

In May 1965 Maharaja Man Singh and Maharani Gayatri Devi completed twenty-five years of marriage. The Maharani who by then had become a successful politician could not travel with her husband as often as she wanted to. Given the Maharaja's love for polo and his formidable reputation as one of the best players in the world he was invited to Cannes that year to help revive polo there. On 9 May 1965 friends invited them to a casino to celebrate their silver wedding anniversary.

between, the Maharani visited India frequently for her party's election campaigns.

In 1967, it was time again for the general elections. As expected, the Maharani won again but her party did not win a clear majority because they didn't contest for all the seats. They could only form a coalition government.

Both Maharaja Man Singh and Maharani Gayatri Devi went to meet Dr Radhakrishnan, the President of India and apprised him of the details. He assured them that they would be given a chance to prove their majority but in an unexpected turn of events, President's Rule was imposed in the state, and then the Congress Party was asked to form the government. The disgruntled public took to the streets in

protest. A curfew was imposed on the entire city of Jaipur and there were violent scenes in the streets culminating in firing that left nine people dead. Maharani Gayatri Devi saw the murkier side of politics and noted in her diary on 9 January 1967: 'Nepotism and corruption have reached the limit and even beyond the limit if that makes sense and the victims as always are the innocent poor. And this from a party that claims to be socialist! It is ironical, sad and heartbreaking to see what is happening to the wonderful people who are Indians. Proud good people sacrificed for the greed and lust of a few. Justice does not exist. Truth is a thing to laugh at. Honesty is a fool. But hunger and want are real. If ever I give up politics it will be because it hurts so much to see all this. I could easily lose myself in the pleasures of travel and international society and bury my head like an ostrich and not look at what is happening but I love too much and too deeply. I love

these people. I love those children. I want a bright future for them. They are India.'

Rao Narpat Singh Baghera, who worked closely with Rajmata as Secretary of the Swatantra Party, points out that besides being a politician and an educationist, she has also worked immensely towards the promotion of local crafts. It was her personal interest that helped revive a dying craft like blue pottery. She introduced new designs in hand block printing in Sanganer as well as Bagru, the two main printing centres around Jaipur.

He says, 'Not many seem to remember that she set up the Shri Ram Shilp Kala Mandir and invited traditional blue pottery craftsmen to train many more new potters. Today, Jaipur is the main centre not only of art and crafts but of the tourism industry as well. In the late sixties and early seventies there was really no concept of promoting these crafts to promote tourism. She really was a pioneer of her time.'

Maharani Gayatri Devi lost two of her family members before making a mark as a politician. Elder sister Ila Devi passed away in 1945. A few years later in 1951 her second brother Maharaj Kumar Indrajitendra Narayan too was gone. But she lost three close relatives

Maharaja Man Singh passes away.

The entire city of Jaipur was plunged in grief after receiving the tragic news of the death of their beloved Maharaja.

in quick succession after she joined politics. Ma Cooch Behar died on 12 September 1968, and her favourite brother Maharaja Jagaddipendra Narayan, Bhaiya, passed away on 11 April 1970. Barely had she recovered from the latest shock that she received another blow—on 24 June 1970 Maharaja Man Singh had a massive heart attack and died while playing polo in England. It was a tragedy that changed her life forever. From Maharani Gayatri Devi she was elevated to the status of Rajmata (Queen Mother) and her eldest stepson Maharaj Bhawani Singh became the Maharaja of Jaipur. 'I could never come to terms with that loss. I was so used to going to him for advice that when he was not there any more I was bereft.'

An entry in her diary dated 10 March 1971 reads: 'I need someone older than me, someone who cares for me. You had such high principles; no one else seems to have those standards. I am lost and miserable without you ... In less than two years I have lost Ma, Dada and you. Life is so cruel, I had so much happiness and love and now nothing.'

Mrs Indira Gandhi was going to cause another major upheaval in her life.

The funeral procession.

The people of Jaipur bid a solemn and tearful farewell to their departed Maharaja

109

In and After Tihar Jail

In a contest between power and patience, bet on patience.

—W.B. Prescott

In 1975 came another dark period in her eventful life, one that shocked and caused great distress to the people in and outside the country. A state of Emergency was declared in India in 1975 and income tax raids were carried out on prominent people—mainly industrialists and opposition leaders. It was not long before the Jaipur royal family found itself in some kind of trouble. Rajmata was living in the hilltop palace, Moti Doongri at that time. Tax officials had paid an unexpected visit there in the hope of finding some incriminating evidence. After hours of rummaging through her personal belongings, they had to make do with a handful of English currency notes on her dressing table. No charges were ever framed against her but she knew it was a matter of time before she was arrested. A few days later when she was in Delhi, she was arrested, and had to spend five months in Tihar Jail under the COFEPOSA (Conservation of Foreign Exchange and Prevention of Smuggling Activities Act).

She still remembers that fateful day, 'It is difficult to ever forget that afternoon on 30 July when I was woken up from my siesta at 33, Aurangzeb Road, New Delhi by one of the staff who came to tell me that two police inspectors wanted to see me. I went to the sitting room

FACING PAGE:

Forever graceful.

Rajmata poses for a Japanese photographer at Lilypool.

111

and they asked me if I was Rajmata Gayatri Devi and when I said, "Yes" they promptly produced a warrant for detention under COFEPOSA. I protested saying that there must be a mistake but they said those were their orders and I must come at once. I went to Bubbles' room to ask for a suitcase and he said, "You've just arrived, where are you going now?" I said, "Bubbles, I'm going to jail because two policemen have come to arrest me." He said, "What nonsense!" I said "No, it's true!" He came into the sitting room with me and they asked him if he was Brigadier Bhawani Singh and they said they had a warrant for his arrest too. We were both speechless. Bubbles asked if we could make a phone call but they refused us that.'

From the lap of luxury Rajmata suddenly found herself in jail with prostitutes and criminals, confined to a small stinking cell.

People were saddened not only by her plight but also because of the unfairness of it all. Letters poured in from all over the world pleading Rajmata's case but Mrs Gandhi remained unmoved.

Looking back now Rajmata doesn't think those days were really all that bad. 'After Bubbles and I arrived at Tihar, the jail superintendent offered us tea and asked us to ring up home and organize bed linen. He was more distressed than we were and tried to do his best for us. Bubbles had quite a decent room with an attached bathroom. My room was not bad either. In fact, the superintendent requested me to help him organize Rajmata Vijayaraje Scindia's room where she was expected to arrive.'

Rajmata maintained a diary in jail and noted each little incident in that. Family members took turns to visit her and Brigadier Bhawani Singh at Tihar Jail. It was a period of great distress for everybody.

'Joey stayed in Delhi throughout. He kept trying to secure our release. We were allowed two visits a week and Bubbles said that Joey should meet us separately; so poor Joey had to come to Tihar Jail four times a week!' Elsewhere in her diary she wrote: 'There is deep pain in my heart—it hurts very much and there is no one to talk to. In the world where I live there is no love, no sympathy, no loving arms, no shoulder to cry on. You have to hide the hurt because if people saw it they would laugh and be pleased. There is no sympathy here, nor any understanding. So all my pent up feelings are hurting and there is a pain in my chest—sometimes it is such an acute pain.'

Her grit and spirit never waned, and she never carried her pain and tears into public space. When she appeared outside the cell and met with other people she was composed and controlled. The other inmates knew her as a brave and strong Maharani who was always there to help and advise them. She lived through the experience with her usual good humour with no outwardly signs of her inner turmoil. She even tried to cheer herself and Rajmata Vijayaraje Scindia of Gwalior, with some humour trying to tide over their bleak and dreary days. In the evenings all the prisoners would shout anti-Mrs Gandhi slogans and Rajmata too would join in!

Urvashi Devi Baria, her granddaughter, recalls, 'We were only allowed to see her once in two weeks so we took turns to visit her. Once my two-year-old son accompanied me and on seeing the iron bars he asked, "Have we come to a zoo?" Grandmother responded immediately, "Yes, it is a zoo. Come in and I'll show you all the animals!" It must have been terrible for her and we just hated what she was being put through but she was very brave and tried instead to cheer us up.'

Her 156-day ordeal came to an end when it was diagnosed that she had stones in her gall bladder and had to be hospitalized. She had

to be operated upon and was still on parole when she left for Bombay.

After her eventual release from Tihar Jail she withdrew from public life for a few months. She kept a low profile and concentrated on her schools and other social service activities. When she returned to Jaipur, the celebrations were rather subdued such was the fear of Emergency. To date she does not like to talk about those stressful days.

Despite being in the public eye for so many years as a politician she regrets having joined politics. She says politics kept her away from her husband and her son. Jagat, her only child, was almost

always on his own and had to do without his mother for long spells because she was away campaigning for her party.

After his initial schooling in India he was sent off to England for further studies. Jagat was a very good-looking boy and he grew up to be a handsome young man. He was a very affectionate child and popular amongst his friends. He idolized both his parents and shared a good relationship with all his stepbrothers. Somehow he never recovered from the loss of his father and this impacted his other relationships as well. He seemed to drift for a while until he met Priya, a Thai princess and married her. Friends hoped that this marriage would do him some good but that was not to be. In the beginning

A reluctant chef.

Though Rajmata has never been fond of cooking, she did try her hand at it during picnics. Here she is helping out in the kitchen at her home in England.

everything was all right. Jagat and Priya divided their time between Thailand and Jaipur. Unfortunately differences cropped up between them and the marriage didn't last. Priya decided that she wanted to go back to Thailand with their two children—Devraj and Lalitya. Jagat was totally devoted to his children and wrote letters to them and sent them presents on their birthday but didn't get to see them for years.

Rajmata wonders if life for Jagat would have been different had she spent more time with him. Perhaps he would have grown up to be a different person, perhaps his marriage wouldn't have broken up and she would still have his children living with her. His horoscope had predicted great things for him were he to live beyond fifty but such was not to be. Jagat died in 1997, at the age of forty-eight after a liver ailment. The months that followed saw Rajmata rather depressed. She talked of death and of having lived too long.

'It was a terrible loss when my beloved, darling son Jagat passed away. It is something that I cannot get over. And I often wonder had I taken more care of him he might still have been with us today. He was such a good-looking, charming, intelligent person and very popular with everybody. He was also generous to a fault. Unfortunately, he had a lot of unhappiness after his marriage broke up. He was not allowed to see or communicate with his children who were the most important part of his life and he missed them terribly. The pain of not being able to meet them is what led to his deterioration. He took to drinking to offset his unhappiness and in the end this caused a liver problem and eventually his death. I shall never forget seeing him lying on his bed in the hospital, not breathing and I knew Jagat was no more. I cannot describe the pain of that moment and every now and then it comes back and I blame myself and I wonder about life and death.'

In 1977 there was a change of government and Rajmata was nominated the chairperson of Rajasthan Tourism Development Corporation. She took her role very seriously trying to do whatever she could to improve the staid and synthetic look of the tourist

FACING PAGE:

A beautiful mind.

Rajmata has espoused a number of social causes in the past, and was singularly responsible for bringing women out of the purdah in a tradition-bound state like Rajasthan. Appalled by the horror of the recent Iraq war, she has volunteered to pay for the treatment of twelve-year-old Ali Ismail Abbas who lost two limbs and his entire family in the war.

bungalows that came under her purview. 'I was the cheapest chairperson that RTDC has ever had. I just cost them a lakh of rupees for the entire year that I held the post. Now people are spending much more every *month!'* smiles Rajmata.

Given her innate sense of style, the interiors of these tourist bungalows seemed very tacky to her. She knew fully well that she was dealing with people who did not have a clue about interior decoration or proper use of space.

'I wasn't trying to turn these bungalows into palaces but sometimes there were little things that only needed a bit of common sense. Simple things like placing doormats and side tables, getting the right curtains and a proper whitewash also became an uphill task. I wasn't being too critical but sometimes it did seem quite frustrating trying to get these basic jobs understood,' she remembers.

Life Now

A man never stands as tall as
when he kneels to help a child.

—Knights of Pythagoras

R ajmata has led a full life with few regrets. If she were to live again she says she would like to be reborn as Maharani Gayatri Devi of Jaipur. She is a much interviewed, photographed and written-about lady even today and could have spent the rest of her life on past glory. But she has chosen to live by the lofty motto of her school 'Our Utmost For The Highest.'

Today, she lives in a small but stylish bungalow, Lilypool, adjoining the Rambagh Palace. The rooms have a wonderful collection of paintings, portraits, silver-framed photographs of her family and other bric-à-brac collected over the years. Her office, where she spends the better part of the morning, is also full of family photographs, rare books and portraits of horses.

Over the years she has started two more schools—the Maharaja Sawai Man Singh Vidyalaya and Lalitya Bal Niketan in a small village outside Jaipur for the villagers. She organizes fund-raising events to run her charitable organization—Sawai Jai Singh Benevolent Trust that helps the poor and needy of the erstwhile Jaipur State. She uses her rich and influential friends overseas to raise funds for causes dear to her heart. Several schools for the handicapped and institutions for the needy have benefited from her philanthropic activities.

She is a much-loved family elder. Her stepsons, Pat and Joey Bapji, live in Jaipur and visit her very often. Rani Vidya Jai Singh, Joey

FACING PAGE:

Of vintage stock.

A lot of cars owned by the Jaipur family were regularly entered in vintage car rallies where they bagged most of the awards. Here Rajmata poses with the Bentley, one of her favourite cars. It still occupies a special place in her garage at Lilypool.

119

Bapji's wife is invaluable for Rajmata as she helps manage all the three schools. Younger sister Menaka Devi, the Rajmata Sahib of Dewas is also a regular visitor. Urvashi Devi (Bambi), Devika Devi and nephew Habi Burman are amongst the various relatives who keep in touch. Honey, the Maharani Sahib of Kota, her brother's daughter remembers how protective Rajmata was towards her when she was growing up. 'I lost my father when I was very young and it was *Pishima* (paternal aunt) who kept a watchful eye over me.'

Habi Burman, her sister Ila Devi's son, married to Moon Moon Sen, remembers her as an affectionate aunt who was always there on their special occasions. She never missed birthdays, engagements, weddings or other family get-togethers. He recalls, '*Mashima* (maternal aunt) has always kept in touch with us and always remembers our birthdays and anniversaries. She never forgets to send cards and gifts on appropriate occasions.'

Friends from England visit her during the winter months. Rajmata dotes on her grandchildren Devraj and Lalitya but does not get to see enough of them.

She now wants to clear the mess created by the property cases that members of the family have slapped against each other. She says, 'I want Jagat's children to be able to look after their property. I have lived a full life, I have no regrets. I have done whatever I wanted to do but I want to tidy up everything before I leave.'

Her days are spent attending to the affairs of the schools and meeting a constant stream of visitors at her office in Lilypool. Old retainers from the days of the State visit her during the first week of every month to collect their pension and to sometimes take personal loans.

The passing years have caused a rift between her eldest son Maharaja Brigadier Bhawani Singh and her, and she is saddened by it. She just says, 'I wish we did not have this tension between us because we were a very close family.'

Her day begins with a puja and some light exercises. Then she comes down to her office in Lilypool. She has a stud farm adjoining

Lilypool with 25 racehorses that are being trained and likes to visit the stud farm every evening and feed the horses.

There is a lot of pain in her voice when she says, 'The city was such a joy to behold. Its architecture was unique. His Highness once told me that whatever we are, we are because of Jaipur and whatever we have we must give back to Jaipur. Times have changed. He has gone. Jagat too has gone, but I am still here and I try my best to do whatever I can for Jaipur.' She looks sadly at the silver-framed pictures on the side table of her beautifully furnished sitting room. 'It is very heartbreaking for me to see this once beautiful place deteriorating so rapidly in front of my eyes, but it is equally heartbreaking to know that the government has not thought it fit to install a statue of the ruler who did so much for the State. Statues of lesser-known leaders who have no connection with the city, have been put up just about everywhere.'

Rajmata turns eighty.

In keeping with tradition, women gather in the zenana to felicitate Rajmata on her eightieth birthday. To her left are her sister Menaka Devi, and her biographer Dharmendar Kanwar.

121

She recently managed to raise funds to the tune of almost rupees twenty lakhs for an NGO involved in the preservation of the city's heritage. Back in 1960 she had written the first letter on the deterioration of Jaipur to the late Prime Minister Jawaharlal Nehru.

'As soon as the State merged with the Dominion of India they started to knock down the walls of Jaipur. His Highness was away somewhere so I went and told the engineer to stop breaking the gates and walls of Jaipur. The work stopped until some senior engineer asked the workers why they had stopped. When they told him that I had asked them to, he was quite annoyed and said that I had no authority to do so and that they were to continue their work. When I learnt of this I thought to myself that there is only one person who can help me and that is Pandit Nehru because he has a sense of history and he is an enlightened man. So I wrote to him and I got a reply the very next day. He said that what they are doing to Jaipur is a sacrilege and he was going to have it stopped at once. And he did. But who are the people today that you can go to? Nobody. The city is being destroyed by haphazard, unplanned growth. I wish the government would do something to rectify some of the mistakes that have been made over the years. It makes me sad to see such a beautiful city going to rack and ruin.'

She looks on dejectedly. 'Can't someone talk to the minister in charge and ask him to remove the hoardings? Won't the government do anything to save the city?' She wants to be reassured that things will improve even though it is hard to reassure someone who has seen so much deterioration in her lifetime.

Over the last twenty years of our association I have been sharing her concern about the city. In the restoration projects that I had undertaken for the government I sought her advice informally at each step. She accompanied me to each site and was generous with her time and knowledge. One area of particular interest to her was the cremation ground of the Maharanis of Jaipur called Maharani ki Chhatri. She looked at the newly restored grounds and said, 'Now I can select a site for myself.'

Every time she is in the vicinity of Amber, the pain resurfaces in her eyes.

'Second Her Highness had wanted to stay in Amber. I wish His Highness had given her a portion—at least that part would have been well maintained.'

Rajmata is equally attached to her hometown and visits Cooch Behar regularly and takes great interest in welfare activities there for which she also arranges funds. She is a much-loved and respected *Amader Rajkumari*, our princess. On her last trip there she was surrounded by thousands of people wanting to touch her, see her and talk to her. It was an amazing display of love and affection. Although she had a cold and fever, nothing could keep her from meeting the people who had travelled miles to see her. In a function at Bausmari, a small village in Cooch Behar district people sang songs eulogizing her and read out poems in her honour: 'Our luminous Princess of Cooch Behar royal family, now Rajmata of Jaipur. She is born of this soil and clime, with an inextricable tie with the people of Cooch Behar. She is full of milk of human kindness and consideration for people like us. In our beloved Rajmata we still find the flickering glory and fame of those days now gone by.'

Age has ushered in minor problems like painful knees and a spot of vertigo but nothing can keep her away from her daily routine. She

FACING PAGE:

Amader Rajkumari, our princess.

Born of the soil and clime of Cooch Behar, Rajmata has an inextricable tie with its people.

travels regularly, preferring to be in England away from the hot Indian summer. Devika Devi says, 'She's not like other elderly people who are always grumbling about their aches and pains. Not only that she has another very admirable quality—she does not try to stifle other people. She allows you to do your own thing and does not expect her young relatives to spend all their time with her. She has always been very understanding and gave us a lot of freedom to do our own thing.'

In her autumn years, she continues to uphold life. The war in Iraq distressed her and she talked of leading a protest march with other like-minded people. She offered to provide all possible help to a little Iraqi orphan, Ali Ismail Abbas, who lost both his limbs in the mindless bombing. Lending a helping hand has been something that has been a way of life with her. Rita Dev Burman, widow of nephew late Bhim Dev Burman (sister Ila Devi's eldest son who died last year), recalls, 'I don't think she has wasted one minute of her life. She has been to parties, she has had a lot of fun but she has continued to help people. Believe me she does a lot. There are times when she gets cheated but that doesn't stop her from doing things for people. She has a presence and a charisma that overpowers everything else. People stop and look at her even today. She has tremendous guts. Always on the move and doing things. She hasn't just existed she has *lived* every minute of her life. She is a real fighter.'

In a befitting tribute to a living legend, Arisia—the exclusive carat-plus-diamond solitaire collection—has launched a limited-edition collection—'The Arisia Rajmata Gayatri Devi Collection.' The exquisite designs in this collection have been inspired by the Victorian, Edwardian and Mughal periods, and are invariably tied up with legends of a regal past.

The Rajmata painstakingly chose each design in this collection herself, and actually took time out for a photography session at Lilypool, wearing each of these pieces. Her enthusiasm was infectious and the team was absolutely dazzled by her.

Her sense of fun, of trying out new things hasn't waned. She has

Attending a function at Udaipur.
A much-loved family elder,
Rajmata never misses birthdays,
engagements, weddings or other
family get-togethers.

an almost childlike interest in whatever goes on around her. A new coffee shop or a pub in town and she is keen to see it or hear about it. Friends remember how she recently went to a jeweller's new house because she found it very interesting while driving past it one day.

For the jeweller, this was indeed an unexpected visit!

The journey has been a long and eventful one. The passing years have etched delicate lines across her face but her inimitable style, grac and inner beauty only reaffirm her unshakeable belief in life.

Epilogue

From Rambagh to Raj Mahal, then to Lilypool, a lot of changes have taken place in my life and in the country. Life is not as glamorous and exciting as it used to be in the olden days. Now I divide my time between India and England. I go to England in summer when it gets very hot here. I leave in May and come back in August just after the rains when everything looks green again instead of dry and dusty, in time for the annual day of both my schools—Maharani Gayatri Devi Girls School and Maharaja Sawai Man Singh Vidyalaya.

I have been fortunate in living the kind of life that I have lived and I understand what the late His Highness meant when he said that whatever we are is because of this city. I want to give something back to the city. Today the people of Jaipur no longer know what a beautiful city it was and how the rulers planned every little aspect of it. It is such a shame to see all these high-rise buildings and hoardings marring the beautiful skyline. I have seen the best years of Jaipur and I do not have very long to live but I want the government, and the people of this city to try and save whatever they can before it is too late.

Another unfinished dream is to see the installation of the late His Highness' statue in Jaipur. He was truly a ruler, the founder of modern Jaipur, who did so much for the city. Yet the government has not thought it fit to install his statue.

Sometimes I feel my time has come. Most of my relatives and dear friends are gone. Many have become old and infirm, and with so many others, I have lost touch. Life goes on. After my previous book *A Princess Remembers: The Memoirs of the Maharani of Jaipur* I did not think there was need for another book on my life. Roli Books, the publishers and Dharmendar Kanwar, my biographer, however, thought otherwise.

FACING PAGE:

Regal forever.

Rajmata at Lilypool during the photo shoot for 'The Arisia Rajmata Gayatri Devi Collection.'

I recall she had first come to meet me in the late seventies in connection with a writing assignment given to her by the late Miss L.G. Lutter, Principal, Maharani Gayatri Devi Girls School. I must admit though that I don't remember much about that assignment.

Since she had a keen interest in writing, in 1979 I asked her to help me compile the late His Highness' biography. She worked diligently on that for a year, meeting people and interviewing them but for several reasons we had to abandon that project.

In 1987 Dharmendar started working for an NGO involved in restoration works in and around Jaipur. Her involvement was very extensive. And since I am very interested in the preservation of old monuments I was delighted that she was able to keep me well informed about the government's plans in these areas. She took me to Nahargarh and Maharani ki Chhatri to see the restoration work and I was indeed very pleased to see for myself the way in which she had supervised the works. In 1999 I asked her to edit my cookbook *Gourmet's Gateway* and was pleased with how the book had shaped up.

She was educated at the Maharani Gayatri Devi Girls School and I am pleased that an alumnus of this school has distinguished herself. To most people today she is known as 'The Quiet Face of Heritage'. To me, however, she has been a wonderful and reliable confidante.

Rajmata Gayatri Devi of Jaipur